Not This
and Other Teachings
from the Spiritual Heart

By
Michael Kewley
Dhammachariya Paññadipa

All rights reserved.

No part of this publication may be reproduced, stored in a retrieval system or transmitted, in any form or by any means, electronic, mechanical, photocopying, recording or otherwise, without prior permission of the publishers.

This book is sold subject to the condition that it shall not by way of trade or otherwise, be lent, re-sold, hired out or otherwise circulated without the publisher's prior consent in any form of binding cover other than that in which it is published and without similar condition including this condition being imposed on the subsequent purchaser.

Copyright © Michael Kewley 1999
ISBN: 978-1-899417-15-5
Revised edition 2013

Published by:
Panna Dipa Books.

E-mail:
dhammateacher@hotmail.com

Typeset & cover design by
Isabelle Kewley

Introduction to this revised edition

Many years ago, at the end of another long and intensive meditation retreat with my teacher, I went to his room with my usual end of retreat question. I knelt before him with my hands together in anjali, the Buddhist attitude of respect and gratitude and asked 'Bhante, how can I improve my practice?' He looked at me for a moment before replying, "Ah, Michael, now you must teach."
This was a shock and certainly not the response I had expected.
The idea of teaching others was something that had never entered my mind and I considered myself only to be a disciple of a teacher, never the teacher himself.
It occurred to me that I had misheard the answer and so I repeated my question.
The response was the same, "Ah, Michael, now you must teach."
With all the humility I could gather, I explained clearly and precisely exactly why I could not be the teacher.
He listened for a moment and then replied, "I do not ask you for you. I ask you for the people who live on your island[1], so that they too might hear the Dhamma."
With such a response how could I refuse?
As with all things from my teacher it was in the service of others. This was not about me, it was only about the continuation of Dhamma.

Thus, slowly and carefully, I began my new life as a Dhamma teacher, although I still insist that I have nothing to teach,

---

[1] Isle of Man, British Isles.

and in fact, Dhamma itself cannot be taught. At best we can share our joy of life, our liberation from fear and our freedom from suffering, but the person called the teacher is nobody.

We can only be the finger that points to the moon but never the moon itself. In the process of pure Dhamma each person must make their own effort, teachers only point the way.

I began to travel, responding to the many generous invitations offered and sharing this beautiful Dhamma as best I could. After some time I was asked to put my Dhamma talks into print so that people could be reminded of our time together.

Again reluctantly, I began to do so, and what you hold in your hand now is a revised edition of the second collection of these talks.

The Buddha reminds us that the Dhamma talk should rouse and inspire the heart of the disciple. If I have achieved this with my words then I am happy. If I have not achieved this I ask for your pardon, for my intention is only to offer the profound joy and beauty of Dhamma. The rest is up to you.

May all beings be happy

Michael Kewley
Dhammachariya Paññadipa
Mirepoix, France
November 2012

Foreword

I have known Michael both as a teacher and a friend since we first met in India in 1992.

As a teacher of Vipassana, Michael is a living example of one who has opened his heart to let the joy of Dhamma shine through.
Vipassana is a beautiful approach to life, an approach where one asks oneself, not the teacher or the practice, 'How do I live my life?'
It is a process of opening our own spiritual heart to live fully and profoundly in the world, sharing the love we realise for ourselves.
Michael is more than the living teacher, because it is not only the words we receive from him, but the very essence of his being, and the essence of his non-being.
His presence, light and loving, sincere and compassionate, is the living proof of his teachings.

As a professional teacher of Tai Chi Chuan, Qi Gong and meditation, I see Michael as an example to us all, both as a friend and the teacher and his stay in Israel this summer has been enjoyed by myself, my students and the many people he has touched with his loving awareness.

May all enjoy this book and this Dhamma and live in peace and happiness.

Oved Yehezkel
Tai Chi Chuan & Qi Gong Master
Israel - July 1998

Not This

Contents

Introduction

PART ONE - The Dhamma Talks
1. Religion and Dhamma training.
2. Loving kindness.
3. Is that so?
4. Balance.
5. Being ordinary.
6. Living in the past.
7. Loving Awareness.
8. Who will wash the dishes?
9. Open your own treasure house.
10. Insight and belief.
11. Why do we do this?
12. The purpose of meditation.
13. Seeing things as they really are.
14. Being hard on yourself.
15. Not this.
16. Everything is best.
17. Letting go.

PART TWO - A meeting with the Buddha
The beginning.
The journey (1).
The journey (2).
The meeting.

PART THREE
Questions and Answers.

Not This

Introduction

In more than forty years of devoted spiritual practice, I can say that I have been truly blessed by my contact with some of the wisest and most loving teachers and masters it is possible to be with. They took care of me, shouted at me, caressed me, occasionally beat me up (emotionally at least), and most importantly, loved me. To each one I owe the greatest debt of gratitude for revealing to me the way to awaken.
But there is one teacher in particular to whom I owe the development of my heart, Sayadaw Rewata Dhamma, a Burmese Buddhist monk and Vipassana master of international repute. This quiet, humble and joyful man showed me not only the power of Vipassana, but also the inescapable importance of love. If I can quote him as ever saying one thing to me in our thirty year relationship, it would be, 'Michael, now you need loving kindness'.
Whenever I would go to his room to complain about my life, how unfair it seemed, how wrong things were for me or for others, he would always say the same thing, 'Michael, now you need loving kindness,' and he was always right!
Because he was my teacher (and still is, even now he is dead) and because I wanted to awaken to truth more than anything else in life, I would always listen with an open heart and then practice what I had heard. It never failed. It is the truth of Vipassana and Metta Bhavana (Awareness and Loving Kindness meditation), the way to peace and happiness.
Of course it wasn't always easy, but I persevered. I lived a life around the beautiful teachings of the Buddha, Zen Masters and Gandhi, people who had cultivated what I wanted most, an open, loving and kind heart.
I began to realise through my own experience that love is not weak, it is real strength. The perfect balance of love

and wisdom does not cultivate the mentality of a victim, blaming others for our experience of unhappiness, but rather it develops confidence and personal power. With wisdom, we know how to live for ourselves. With love we do not insist that others follow our way.
Love and awareness are the most important requirements of spiritual development, for without them we cannot ever proceed beyond the limitations we place upon ourselves. To open our heart and allow love and wisdom to flow freely, spontaneously and without limit is truly a blessing for ourselves and ultimately all beings.

Now myself a teacher of Dhamma, leading intensive courses throughout the world, I make a point of introducing the loving kindness practice as early as possible, rather than as is in the Vipassana tradition, on the final morning. It is always the longest explanation of a practice that I give and is always followed by an evening Dhamma talk on how to take this practice into our daily life. To sit in meditation with loving kindness is never enough, we must use it in every moment and in every situation.
Love and awareness are not things we add to our lives like a new hobby or pastime, they are the place from where we begin to live our life.

They are the opening of the spiritual heart.

May you find the Dhamma contained in this book
beneficial for your life.
May you experience true joy and happiness
manifesting from your heart.
May all beings, no matter who, no matter where,
benefit from your loving journey.

PART ONE

The Dhamma Talks

Not This

1 - Religion and Dhamma training

*'We turn away from openness
and close ourselves to anything
that is not part of our own conditioning.'*

A man died and went to heaven. Upon arrival he was given a guided tour by St Peter, who pointed out the different groups of people sitting quietly and happily together.
"Over there are the Hindus," said St. Peter, "and there are the Buddhists and here are the Muslims," and so on.
Eventually they came to a great walled area from behind which came music and singing and cheering.
"Who is in there?" asked the man.
"Oh don't worry about them," said St Peter, "that's the Christians - they think they're the only ones up here!"

There is a common misunderstanding that religion and Dhamma training are the same thing. This may sometimes appear to be true, but in reality they are generally opposed to each other. In worldly understanding religion means to believe in something. To have faith and conviction in a particular set of ideas and values and accept them as being completely true. Whatever religion you follow, your beliefs are clearly marked out and you know who and what you are. The Christians believe that Jesus is the son of God, and only through belief and faith in him can salvation be attained. This position is unalterable and not only has to be proclaimed to the world, but constantly defended as being the only truth. However, the Jews feel the same about their religion, as do the Muslims and Hindus and everyone else. We all believe that the religion we follow is the only true way, even if in

modern times we do pay lip service to the merits of other beliefs.
Religion means to be closed-minded, to exclude other possibilities as having any real value. It is not only Christians who feel this way. It is the same for all religions.

There was once a nun who lived at a certain monastery in Japan. She was very devoted to the Buddha and her practice of Buddhism. One day whilst she was meditating, she had an idea to make a clay image of the Buddha on which to focus her attention.
This she did. She took care with her work and when her small statue was finished she covered it with gold leaf. The nun was very pleased with the appearance of her statue and took it to the temple in preparation for the evening meditation. Lighting some incense beneath it she began her practice. However, she noticed that the incense was not only reaching her Buddha statue, but because of the slight draught in the temple, was drifting in many directions, and so touching all the other statues. This she did not like!
Instantly, the nun had an idea to remedy this. She would make a funnel so that the fragrance from her incense would reach only her statue and not spread throughout the whole temple and so be shared with the other Buddha statues.
The next time the meditation was called she was ready. She positioned the funnel above her incense and directed it towards her statue. Having lit the incense and watched the smoke drift up the funnel, she began to meditate.
At the end of the session when the bell was sounded the nun opened her eyes to gaze upon her beautiful statue. However, what she saw horrified her! The smoke from her incense, directed to reach only her own Buddha statue, had blackened its face, making it completely ugly.

This is the way religion usually works. As we become more self-absorbed in our own traditions and beliefs, we also become more narrow-minded and intolerant to the views of others. We turn away from openness and close ourselves to anything that is not part of our own conditioning.
Actually, it's very interesting.
We simply believe things we have been told. It's not as though we have had any direct experience of the nature of our belief. It's just a habit. It's just conditioning.
If we had been born in India, we would be a Hindu or a Muslim or a Sikh and completely conditioned by those particular beliefs and traditions.

Religion has the value of organising society, of creating rules and social conventions that the greatest number of people can live by. It establishes order and control.
Order and control is how society functions. This is what religion creates and why it is opposed to true Dhamma training.

In the 1970's a famous Buddhist monk and Vipassana master was invited to meet with some of the Christian clergy in England.
During their meeting, the monk was asked the question, "Is the Buddhist truth the same as the Christian truth, or is it different?"
The monk smiled and answered simply, "How can there be more than one truth?"

Dhamma training is never about accepting things at face value or believing what others tell us. It is about discovering for ourselves, the universality of truth. It is a direct process of investigation, discovery and realisation. It is not an easy road of blind faith and belief. It is swimming against the current and going against what has been well established.

Religion provides something for the masses. It provides rituals and conventions. It tells people who and what they are and what they must believe. From that comes the structure of society.

Dhamma training reminds us that nothing is the way it seems to be – nor is it otherwise, and if you truly want to understand reality in a direct and immediate way, you have to let go of all your preconceived views and opinions as to how things are.

You have to be open.

You have to be open to the possibility that everything you have accepted for all these years as being the truth is actually nonsense. That it is just conditioning.

Dhamma training means to take a new perspective on life and existence itself. Where we no longer cling to the past and to the idea that only we know the truth of the universe. It is rather the opposite. It is that actually we don't know how things are, we only know what we have been told and that no matter how many views and opinions we may form and no matter how valid they may seem at the time, without the wisdom gained through our own direct experience of truth they are still only ideas, either our own, or worse, someone else's.

Religion has its value but it's not the truth.

Let go of religion. Let go of blind faith. Let go of everything that tells you who and what you are and you will arrive at the point of freedom and realise liberation from the limitations that we place upon ourselves. And just when you think that there is nothing else to let go of, let go of that too!

All masters face the same obstacles.
The purpose of the master is to point to the truth, but point is all they can do. They cannot realise the truth for another. They can push, support, encourage and even bully their disciples into making an effort with the practice, but they cannot do the practice for them. This is very important to understand. To realise the truth, we have to make the effort ourselves.

Even the value of the master, no matter who it may be, is extremely limited.
Siddhartha Gotama, the Buddha, my personal hero in life and founder of what is now known as the Vipassana or Insight system of meditation, was very clear on this point;

> Purity and impurity are personal concerns.
> No-one can purify another.

> Dhammapada: verse 165

However, when sharing Dhamma, all masters face the same obstacles to the realisation of the truth and that obstacle is the mind of the student.
To speak in general terms we can say that for the new student to Dhamma practice, the mind is generally preoccupied with the two extremes of superstition (belief) and the intellect (thinking). Our educational system is based upon acquiring more and more information about more and more things and the simplistic idea of filling an empty brain to capacity. The

result is a mind that cannot be still but needs to think and speculate about everything!

So when I tell you to 'let go,' you find it very hard, some may even say impossible, and the reason is simple. You have all read too much, you have all thought too much. You have all spent too much time trying to work everything out with the intellect, and not enough time - if any - 'simply being.'
This is a tragedy in life, especially when we realise that we only believe or disbelieve what we have read or heard. If something conforms to our own personal views, we accept it. If it doesn't conform to our personal views we reject it. In any case, the result is the same. Taking a position for or against and formulating an opinion about something we haven't actually experienced for ourselves!

I don't ask you to believe my words. I ask you to examine them, to reflect upon what I say with an open mind. The truth is not something we can form an opinion about.
Truth is truth. That is all.
Leave a space in your mind for every possibility.

Closing the mind through the formation of views, opinions and beliefs prevents us from experiencing the wonderous possibilities of life. As long as you empower even the smallest belief, you limit yourself. Don't do it!

Stay open. Be true to yourself, however that is.

There is a tribe of Indians in South America, who refuse to fence their fields. They say that to put a fence around their fields is to put a fence around their minds - to lose their freedom.

Freedom is not something that comes from doing just what you want, whenever you want to, although this is the popular view. Freedom comes from not being a prisoner of your own beliefs and conditioning.
There is nothing that you really are and no set pattern to which you have to adhere to. Don't limit yourself by belief.

Belief is not the truth. Belief is what we cultivate when we don't know the truth.

Views and opinions about how things should be for ourselves and others and of how society and the world should behave are just more traps of the mind. Let them go, let them all go. In letting go, we truly liberate ourselves and so realise freedom.
It is only conceit to feel that we must have an opinion about everyone and everything. It is enough to say 'I don't know' and remain open to the infinite possibilities of life.

Religion is about conforming and being part of a larger group. Dhamma practice is about going solo, taking responsibility for yourself. It is about swimming against the tide of popular belief and conformity and discovering the truth of your own reality for yourself. Empowering love and wisdom in every moment and being free from delusion, whatever form it may take.

2 - Loving kindness

*'If our practice is not making us happier,
how is it helping us?'*

At one time there was a monk who was very intent on practice. Every day he would sit for long hours in meditation, always beginning before everyone else and always finishing later. His whole practice revolved around meditation. One day the Master of the monastery where the monk was living saw him in the temple meditating and asked him what he was doing.
"I am meditating to become enlightened," said the monk.
The Master smiled and went outside. He picked up a small stone from the garden, entered the meditation hall again and sat down next the monk. Here he began to rub the stone on his robe. At first the meditating monk paid no attention, but finally his curiosity got the better of him and he opened his eyes.
"What are you doing?" he asked the Master.
"I am polishing this stone to produce a diamond," answered the Master.
"How can polishing a stone produce a diamond?" asked the monk.
"How can sitting in meditation produce enlightenment?" replied the Master.

In my years of sharing Dhamma in India, America and Europe I have met many people who were also very intent on their meditation practice. However, like the monk in the story, their intentions were not pure. They all wanted a return on their practice. Enlightenment, special abilities, recognition or a good rebirth at the very least. To this end,

they were applying many different teachings from many different traditions, about which they seemed to know little. But they did practice and the results seemed to be lots and lots of people doing lots and lots of things that they thought would do them some good!
This of course is natural. This is why we begin a spiritual life, to get something out of it. Something we think will do us some good.
Even if our motive is so high-minded as to want something for ourselves that ultimately will help many beings, if a goal is in mind, our intentions are not pure.
In the Buddhist schools in Zen and Theravada once we find a teacher, we are told to meditate. Meditate, meditate and meditate some more. Hour upon endless hour of sitting cross-legged on the floor, watching the breath in the nostrils, feeling the sensations in the body and fighting pain, sleepiness and boredom. However, we believe that if we want liberation or enlightenment this is the way to get it.
As long as we don't know what these things are, we formulate opinions about them.
Opinions and belief.
After some time, if we are aware, we may begin to realise that even after hundreds of hours of sitting meditation practice we haven't actually become free or enlightened. In fact, nothing very much has happened. However, perhaps we recognise that the practice itself does have a certain quality about it and so for that reason alone, we continue. Now we no longer seek the results of practice, we practice for its own sake. This is the moment of change, this is when enlightenment and true liberation can be realised.

People, as we know, are result oriented. From our earliest days at school, competition and the sense of achievement is reinforced into our way of thinking. Because of this early conditioning, it is only natural that we should take these attitudes into all aspects of life. Why should it seem unreasonable for meditation and other spiritual practices to produce specific results? However, it is because of this attitude that we actually try too hard.

We attend talks, sit for hours in meditation and try to understand everything at once. The depth of meaning behind spiritual matters is so vast, how can we expect to know it all immediately? However, what we don't understand fully we are always happy to formulate views and opinions about. We organise everything neatly in our mind to suit our own level of understanding.

Many people struggle, trying to understand the things that they have heard. Sometimes this is due to the way that the teaching is given and other times it is simply because it is beyond the scope of that particular person at that time. However, for whatever reason, the result is a feeling of unhappiness, manifesting as a sense of failure and inadequacy.

In all walks of life, and perhaps especially in spiritual practice, this attitude is counter-productive.

The attitude that I noticed about these people was that they had no loving kindness towards themselves.

The first thing we have to understand is the value of practice. If our practice isn't making us happier, how is it helping us? Outside spiritual training, when we feel happy we share that feeling with others. We have energy and an outward going attitude. A generous feeling towards helping others. How much more so in the spiritual life? However, if we are miserable and unhappy, we tend to keep ourselves to ourselves and not want to mix with others. We want to be

left alone to wallow in our own negative mental states. No difference here between the spiritual life and ordinary life.
It is a profound Dhammic truth that we have to understand the point of practice.

We can say that the purpose of practice is to open the spiritual heart. The spiritual heart is like a rose, whose petals have not yet opened. With wisdom these petals will unfold and the beautiful fragrance can be enjoyed by all. These beautiful and fragile petals cannot be wrenched open by long hours of intensive practice, even though in the course of spiritual training this can be very valuable, they have to be allowed to unfold naturally. We have to expose the spiritual heart to care and love for ourselves in order to benefit most. We must develop an attitude of gentleness and patience in our practice, each day cultivating our heart through meditation and harmonious living. We must rid ourselves of the burning desire to get somewhere.
If the natural state of mind is already pure, where is it that we want to get to?

Practice is everything, but practice with wrong intention is nothing.

To be gentle with ourselves does not mean to take it easy. It means to be easy. It means to take ourselves as far as we can, and then a little further. But always with the right attitude. With an ungrasping attitude, and a mind that is not always looking at the spiritual scoreboard to see how well it is doing. We want to develop the finer qualities of humanity such as compassion and love, calmness of mind and joyfulness, but we must also know where these qualities begin and end. They do not begin in a mind fraught with frustration or desire to progress and impress, that is where they end. These qualities begin in a mind that is peaceful and a mind that does not fight against itself. The establishment of this mind begins with the right attitude to practice.

It is no secret that what the world needs is love, and as disciples of Dhamma we must establish the way to live in this world harmoniously. However, this very harmony has to begin with ourselves. If we cannot be open and accepting to the faults and failings we see within ourselves, how can we develop peaceful feelings towards the rest of the world?
Before we can accept the many we have to accept the one. Ourselves. Loving ourselves for who we are, what we are, and perhaps most importantly on the spiritual path, where we are, is the key to practice.
Here loving does not mean liking. Loving means to be fully accepting of ourselves as we are in this moment. Not as we would like to be, not as we think we should be, but actually as we are.
To say that we like our negative mental states such as anger or jealousy would be foolish, but from an attitude of love, of complete and unconditional acceptance, we can recognise them as natural impulses of mind and not condemn ourselves for being subject to them.
The attitude of love means that we are able to exist peacefully with everything, even our own mind. This transcends our habitual pattern of liking and disliking, grasping and rejecting and trying to arrange everything in our personal universe to suit ourselves. It means to let go. To relax and enjoy a softer, gentler approach to situations, relationships and life in general.

The practice of removing the taints that obscure the pure

mind, the mind without the qualities of greed, hatred and delusion also has to be entered upon with the right attitude. It is not really feasible for us to determine to eradicate all of our unwholesome qualities and tendencies of mind in one fell swoop, but slowly, slowly with patient and loving practice it can be done.

Often, after an especially calm and peaceful meditation sitting, people may feel that all their habits towards impatience and irritability have been broken, only to find some time later, that they are still there, as strong as ever.

We don't know where these tendencies begin and end within us or how deep they go, but by using the right attitude to practice we can begin to develop some wisdom into how to deal with them.

We don't need to cut off these qualities as a surgeon might amputate a limb, but we can ease them out by no longer providing the fuel for them. Just as a fire, no matter how fierce, if left alone and not fed, will die down and finally go out by itself, so too will the fires of greed, hatred and delusion die down in our heart, until eventually they are extinguished altogether.

As we develop wisdom into seeing how things really are for ourselves, we also begin to understand that it is exactly the same for others. Our mind, and the mind of our fellow human beings, is the same mind, filled with fears, anxieties, desires for self happiness and aversion towards suffering. How we live in the world is simply a reflection of our predominant mental states.

This is a revelation and from this stems true compassion. The recognition that we are all struggling with life, all seeking the same things and all feeling the same pains. It is only the quality of the struggle that is different.

It is necessary to be open to ourselves and others. To be non-judgemental. We don't always know the problems and difficulties that others struggle with, but we know from our own experience that pain, sorrow, anger and disappointment are hard to bear. Once we know this from our practice, the responsibility to help and be of service is always upon us. In Tibetan Buddhism there is the practice of seeking out the one percent that is good or worthy, in a person that is otherwise ninety nine percent despicable.

For me, even this is too much. Better I think, to be totally accepting of the other person as they are, without looking for even the smallest thing that we can approve of.

If we are completely accepting of someone and not making judgements as to whether there is something minutely small worthy of respecting we can be at peace with them, not demanding that they be any different, just to please us.

The purpose of practice is to allow the spiritual heart to open. To live in the world in a way that is of benefit to ourselves and others. To be of use, but not to make demands. To do what is right, because it is right and not for any ulterior motive. Once we live in this way, who can ever offer us blame or criticism. When our intentions are pure, then good results are bound to follow.

3 - Is that so?

'Life itself is practice.'

On the outskirts of a small village in Japan there lived the famous Zen master Hakuin. Because he lived a pure and simple life, he was well respected and supported by the villagers. His way of living was quiet and austere, perfect behaviour for a man of Zen.

One day in the village, the daughter of a local shopkeeper announced that she was pregnant. As she was unmarried, this was disastrous news. Shame rained down on her and her family. At first the girl, out of loyalty, refused to name the father. Her own father threatened her, her mother beat her, even her friends shunned her, such was her disgrace. Her life, already difficult, was becoming impossible. Finally, she weakened.

"It was Hakuin," she cried, "he is the father."

The family were outraged. This 'so-called' man of Zen, could not live without his pleasure. He must pay for his actions.

In a body, they went to his small hut on the outskirts of the village to confront him.

"Our daughter claims that you are responsible for her pregnancy," yelled the father, "what do you say to that?"

Hakuin sat on the small veranda of his hut, and looked towards the girl. She was small, young and afraid.

"Is that so?" was all he said.

The parents, still furious, left Hakuin with a message that as soon as the child was born it would be brought to him and he could take care of it.

"Is that so?" was Hakuin's only response.

In due course, the child was born and brought to Hakuin. His

reputation by this time was in shreds, and only a few people in the village had any time for him at all. The simple villagers, as with most people were quick to believe a scandal.
"As we warned you," said the still angry parents, "we have brought the child for you to look after. This is now your responsibility, we want nothing more to do with it."
"Is that so?" said Hakuin, gently accepting the child and closing the door of his hut.
For one year Hakuin, now seen to be in complete disgrace, cared for the child and attended to it's every need. He obtained food and milk from the few villagers that still had time for him and gave the baby his fullest attention.
Eventually, at the end of the twelfth month, the young mother could bear the situation no more. She broke down and confessed that the father of the child was in fact a young man who worked at the local fish market. She had been afraid of what her parents might do to him, and so had named Hakuin as the father. Again, the family was furious. They had accused a pure living man of Zen of sexual misconduct, ensured that his reputation was all but destroyed and finally thrust their daughters baby on to him to raise alone.
What shame was now on their family? With heads lowered, and in a long procession, they left the village and slowly made their way to Hakuin's hut. Once more, they found Hakuin sitting on the veranda, this time gently rocking the baby in a crude bamboo cradle.
"We have come to apologise, "said the father, "we now know the truth and with your permission we would like to take the baby back to its real family."
Hakuin was willing and as he handed the child to the young mother, he said just three words, "Is that so?"

There is an expression:

If life doesn't turn out exactly as you planned, don't be surprised.

When we reflect upon our life, it is very easy to see how we got to where we are.
We can trace a course backwards in time and identify all the improbable and unlikely things that happened and all the chance encounters and opportunities that we were able to take advantage of. From our perspective of 'now', our journey seems clear and obvious.
If that hadn't occurred, this would not have happened.
However, the future is the great unknown. From this very moment onwards, we do not know what can happen. It may be something pleasant, it may be something unpleasant, but right now we cannot determine either. As we make our journey into the unknown, there are only two paths that we can take:
The path of wisdom or the path of fear.

For most of my early life, I was a planner and an organiser. A person who upon awakening in the morning, will know exactly in their mind how the day will proceed. To have everything planned and organised brings with it the sense of security. The feeling of control.

On one occasion, when I was a very young man, I was helping a friend paint the walls of his new apartment, he turned to me and said, "Oh, you're a square painter!"
A square painter is a person who marks out a certain area of the wall with paint first and then proceeds to fill in that area. Only when that has been done, will he mark off the next area and move on. I was a person like this. Very organised.

When I first went to India I met many people who were definitely not 'square painter's'.

They would start their day only with the vaguest notion of how it would develop, but apart from that everything was left to fate, chance and circumstance. In reality, they left everything to the opportunity of the moment.

"The day will turn out as it turns out," they would tell me.

I, myself, did not like this idea very much and so resisted. A person needs a plan. For their day. For their life.

However, as my stay in India lengthened my way of thinking began to change.

India does that. To be in a place where it can take two hours to buy a train ticket and then that train can be twenty three hours late, has to have an effect. You either go with it or it makes you crazy, the choice is yours.

One's attitude becomes more open and receptive to the unpredictable conditions that life has to offer.

Of course, I could always justify my habit of planning and organising everything by reminding people that when I was married and with my family, somebody had to do it and that somebody was me! In a family situation it is not always practical to simply allow events to unfold in their own way. There has to be an element of control and guidance. Actually, these views are still valid.

To be a part of society, to have a family and to go to work, means that we have to plan and organise. We have to have a routine. This is the way of ordinary life. Even Hakuin would have his routine. A time to wake up in the morning and a time to eat. A time for bathing and a time for sleeping. Routine most definitely has its value. However, this value is undermined when the routine is adhered to rigidly without any appreciation of the unpredictability of everyday life.

When I ordained as a Buddhist monk, the first thing I was presented with was a daily routine. A programme of activity, neatly written and covering the whole day from rising very early in the morning to retiring very late in the evening. Not a single moment was unaccounted for.

"Of course," said my guiding monk, "there may never be a day when you will be able to follow this list from start to finish, but whenever unpredicted interruptions have passed, you will know exactly what you should be doing."

The point was not to follow a list of things to do, only never to be in a position of not knowing what to do next. Not knowing can be extremely dangerous. It can lead us into a lot of trouble. Look at a child when it's bored. It can do anything!

Some years ago, my sister's son awoke early one Sunday morning and having nothing better to do, went downstairs and carved his name into the pine breakfast table. Even he could not understand what made him do it. Obviously, it was not something that would go unnoticed for very long.

Boredom, simply not knowing what to do next, can be a straight road to danger.

So here we have a dilemma. To organise one's thinking and consequently one's life, is to limit oneself to the possibilities that life offers. To adhere rigidly to predetermined plans and schemes will truly blind us to the beauty that uncertainty offers.

If Hakuin had fitted this mould, he would have kicked and screamed when accused of being the father of the child. This was certainly not part of his life's plan, to suddenly and quite unexpectedly find himself as a one parent family. However, the opposite way of thinking, that of randomness and non organisation, is not correct either.

Simply to allow anything to happen, no matter what, also only leads to danger. To only get up when we wake up and to only work when we feel like it may sound very attractive, but in reality is always counter productive.

If Hakuin had cultivated this attitude, he may have simply run away when presented with the prospect of looking after a small baby, not being able to accept the responsibility.

On the other hand, if he had taken on this heavy burden, who knows when the baby would have been fed or changed or laid down to rest?

However, Hakuin's balance was just right, the mark of spiritual master. Each day he would be involved in practice. For him it would be not possible for it to be otherwise. Life itself is practice. Whether walking, sitting, standing or lying down, his mind would be perfectly balanced, observing the natural flow of mental and physical phenomena. In spiritual terms this is called, 'Every moment Dhamma'. The perfect practice of harmony with life.

His day would have its own routine and its own rhythm. When to eat, when to sleep, when to wash and so on. But these would only be a guidance. An outline for daily life, not a set of rules and disciplines to be adhered to blindly.

Hakuin knew that the nature of life is unpredictable. He knew that no matter how much we may want to control everyone and everything we come into contact with, so that they will always be perfect for us, it is impossible.

In reality, none of us know what can happen, even in the next moment. Our fortunes can change as quickly as the winking of an eye and the only way to keep our internal balance in such an unpredictable world is to be open and ready for anything.

If we don't know what is around the corner, how can we plan for it?

The Zen master asked a student, "are you ready?"
"Ready for what?" answered the student.
The master just shook his head and walked away.

This really is the question that we need to ask ourselves. Are we ready? Ready for what?
Ready for life!

At one time there was an old rabbi in Russia, who would cross the town square very early every morning and go to the synagogue. He had been following the same routine every morning for more years than anyone could remember. One morning he was met by a Cossack.
The Cossack had been drinking heavily the night before, had fought with his wife when he returned home, slept on the floor and left home that morning without any breakfast. He was in a bad mood. However, upon seeing the old rabbi crossing the town square he decided, in a moment of friendliness, to greet him.
"Good morning, Rabbi," said the Cossack, "Where are you going?"
"Don't know," said the rabbi.
This curt answer infuriated the Cossack who exploded with rage.
"For more than twenty years you have been crossing the town square at the same time every morning to go to your

synagogue," he yelled, "But today when I ask you where you are going, you tell me that you don't know. Come with me."
The Cossack then roughly took the old rabbi by the scruff of the neck, marched him down to the local jail and promptly threw him into a cell.
He slammed the door closed, and just as he was turning the key in the lock the Cossack looked through the bars to see the old rabbi standing in the middle of the cell smiling at him.
"You see," said the rabbi, "you just don't know."

Hakuin and the old rabbi were completely open to the uncertain and changing conditions of life and were able to flow. To flow with life itself.
When Hakuin was accused of being the father of the child he simply responded, "Is that so?"
No affirmation. No denial. No problem.

With the understanding developed through the practice of Vipassana and Loving Kindness meditation, we will all be more open and flowing with the uncertainties of life.
After all, if we cannot control the things that pass through our mind, how can we control the things that pass through our day?

4 - Balance

*'If we truly want to train ourselves,
we have to stop feeding the ego.'*

At one time there was a master who was approached by a student, complaining of his wife's stinginess. He asked the master if he would speak to her. The master agreed and went to the home of the student and his wife.
He knocked on the door and the instant the wife answered, he held up his fist in front of her face.
"What do you mean by that?" she asked.
"Suppose my hand was always like this," asked the master, "what would you call it?"
"Deformed," said the wife.
The master then released his fist and held his open hand up to her face.
"And if it was always like this?" he asked.
"Another kind of deformity," the wife replied.
"If you understand that much you are a good wife," said the master and went upon his way.
After his visit, the wife helped her husband share as well as save.

One of the qualities of spiritual progress is balance. This is achieved through the establishment of a calm and peaceful centre. Actually, this centre is not acquired by doing anything special, or by developing any particular talents or abilities, but by simply letting go of the minds natural tendency to operate in extremes.
We can see the process of the mind quite clearly in our meditation practice. When a mental state arises it overwhelms

us and we become that thing. Without awareness there is no separation from what we experience and ourselves. We simply become the mental state we are experiencing.

Because of this habit of becoming, we are flung from one extreme position of the mind to the next without rest from the moment we awaken until we fall asleep again. This insidious and habitual activity is exhausting and it is no surprise that we are tired by the end of each day. Without balance we find ourselves on a roller coaster ride that is difficult to get off.

Vipassana meditation is the practice we apply to recognise and understand this never ending process of mind. It is the only way to establish a position of balance, both in our sitting practice and in life. Peacefully accepting the natural movements of the mind as 'not me', 'not mine', 'not what I am', and so no longer be under their influence.

It is as simple as that!

The result of this practice of calm, loving and non-attached observation is peace and harmony, because no matter what extreme feelings or emotions the mind grasps at, from our central position of balance, we are no longer drawn into them. This is how we create a calm and peaceful centre, and how we establish balance within ourselves.

Actually, in Vipassana meditation this is relatively easy to do because of the guidelines regarding our practice. We sit still, without fidgeting or scratching every itch. No longer blindly following every impulse to change our posture the moment we notice even the smallest physical discomfort. We train ourselves to sit still and observe dispassionately.

We allow everything to arise and fall away, thus naturally establishing an attitude of peace and balance. Of being with things 'as they are'.

In everyday life it may not seem such a straightforward affair. So many distractions pulling at our centre. So many choices to be made. It can be very confusing and may seem far, far away from the peace of meditation.
However, we have to remember that Vipassana is not a sitting practice only. It is a living practice and the objects for awareness that arise in the mind are the same for all of us, whether we are in a beautiful Dhamma hall or a busy supermarket on a Saturday afternoon. Wherever we are, whatever situation we find ourselves in, observation of mind and body can continue. The practice itself is not confined to time or place.

However, in the beginning at least, we will always be drawn from our centre into the world of extremes. It is inevitable, but if we are sincere in our training, we will be able to catch ourselves, focus and find our internal balance once again. It takes only a moment.
Centre on the touch sensation of breath in the nostrils, or simply in the predominant feeling in the body. Just go to that sensation for a moment and you're back.
Back in your centre. Back in control.
Balance means peace. It means a mind that is not drawn into the pettiness of life. A mind that does not grasp at things for itself. A mind that is not always complaining.

At one time a student asked me, "How will I know when I'm enlightened?"
I replied, "When you stop complaining about your life."

To be out of balance means to be self obsessed. To see things only from the position of self interest (ego) and so always making choices established in a personal desire for happiness. The ego only ever asks one question of life, "what's in it for me?"

From ego, we always react to a situation with a mind filled with desire or aversion, rather than responding with wisdom and love. To be out of balance means to see events and situations from the limited position of self interest and what we can gain or loose.

With wisdom and balance, we will be able to see clearly that what we call life is not personal. It's just life. Situations and events arising and passing away. Not seeking our permission or consent. Just life.

With ego, we make everything personal, we make everything about us and so suffer the consequences.

The truly spiritual life is a life of releasing our attachment to things. Once we release our attachment to ego, we are free.

With the right attitude we will see that whatever situation we find ourselves in, we can use as an opportunity to train, to develop ourselves so that we are happy and then able to share that happiness with all beings.

However, this takes determination, and for the most part spiritual practice is seen as something we adhere to when things are going well. When life is convenient. It is at times like these when people will say how well their practice is going. By contrast, when they are confronted by anger or unpleasant situations at home or at work, the training is forgotten in the attempt for the ego to redeem itself. Rather than examining the situation from a position of balance, they follow the well-established habit of the mind and jump straight in with their reactions. Later of course, these can always be justified.

Only ego seeks to explain and justify its actions.
If we truly want to train ourselves, we have to stop feeding the ego, that part of us that is always looking for approval and acknowledgement of its actions, and every other kind of praise and glory. To do this we must use the situation we find ourselves in, and not continually seek only the pleasant ones.

So, when we are confronted by the anger of others, rather than simply reacting with the desire to strike out and retaliate, use that moment as a focus for training. Don't feed the ego. Find the point of balance. Learn to let go of these deep-rooted tendencies to be seen by others in a certain light, and simply 'be'. If there is anger in your heart, let it go. If there is fear in your heart, let that go. If there is pain in your heart, let that go. Let everything go. These things do not serve us in any beneficial way and lead only to more and more unhappiness in our life. Don't cling to anything. Don't push anything away. Allow whatever is present to become fully conscious and respond.
Response is something that we do from wisdom. Reaction is always what we do from ignorance.

We can only train ourselves in the moment when we are confronted by different mental states. It is not possible to keep a pledge no matter how noble, never to be angry again. None of us know how deeply rooted anger is within us, or what conditions will trigger its arising. It is only in the moment when it does arise that we can actually see it.
Only then and from a position of balance, can we allow the attachment to anger and all our other mental states to fall away and experience the deeper peace within.
Balance is what we cultivate when we sit in meditation, but our goal of practice must be to take that balance into our

everyday activity and allow it to manifest in every situation.

In our early days of spiritual practice we tend to separate meditation from daily life. We create a division. Work, social events and family life is one thing, but spiritual practice is quite distinctly something else. We keep the two aspects of life quite separate, with meditation usually seen as the antidote to all the stress and pressure we experience simply by living in the world. Actually, this kind of attitude can be quite harmful as long as we see meditation as an escape from ordinary existence.

There was once a grocer who died and went to heaven, where he was met by St Peter.
"I'm sorry, but you can't come in," said St Peter.
"What do you mean?" asked the grocer, "why can't I come in? I went to church every Sunday, I sang in the church choir and I helped with all the church activities. Why can't I come in?"
"Well actually," said St Peter, "you just weren't a very good grocer."

This poor man had made the mistake of dividing his life into two parts, the spiritual and the worldly. He'd lost his balance. Every Sunday he would go to church and hear the beautiful Christian teachings of love, compassion and tolerance. Upon leaving however, he would return to his own world and continue to live a life at the level of a businessman, creating his environment from greed, hatred and delusion, always being involved in the world without awareness or love, and so completely separating himself from his spiritual training. What a waste!
Actually, there is no separation between spiritual life and the

worldly life. Any distinction we may experience exists only in our mind, for in reality one is the proving ground for the other.

To use each and every situation as it presents itself as an opportunity for further development and to recognise the different conditions of mind and their effect in each moment, is the essence of spiritual growth.

To take our meditation sitting and use it as an escape from the world is to misuse the practice completely. Vipassana enforces the habit of balance by constantly returning us to our centre where we always have a clear picture of what is really happening. From our centre of balance, peace and non-judgement we are not deluded by the appearance of things.

The world that we experience is the one we create for ourselves, moment after moment. With balance we can see this truth clearly. To be out of balance means to be lost in the darkness of mind and back in the world, completely caught up in our fantasies of how things should be, and how they should not be.

The mind we face in meditation is not a special mind, something unique to our sitting practice. It is our usual, everyday mind. The one that gets upset, bears a grudge and can't stop thinking. The mind that seeks something special and becomes disappointed and despondent when it doesn't happen.

True meditation is never an escape from the world. It is a real facing of the world. Our world. The world that we create for ourselves. The world that we live in.

From a position of balance we will be able to experience for ourselves, that everything that arises into the mind passes away, and the result of that passing is peace. Into the now spacious mind, anything can arise, and there is no attachment, no judgment, no praise and no condemnation, only perfect acceptance. We let go of the comparing mind, the mind that is always looking for results, for perfect conditions and experience peace. Perfect peace amongst the chaos of mental activity.

This attitude of practice is appropriate in every moment. With understanding we will see that everything is meditation, and meditation is everything.

To continually return to our centre, to our point of balance, means that we are not always being drawn out into the ultimately painful world of ego and the senses, but are in a position to see what is really happening and most importantly, where it is happening.

We all have to face the vicissitudes of life and the mental turmoil they produce, but whenever we remain balanced we will see these situations and the conditioned mind states for what they really are.

Impermanent movements arising and passing away. Like clouds passing through a clear and empty sky.

This is the way to live in the world, to be in balance and to make everything meditation.

5 - Being ordinary

'There is no need to renounce anything.'

There was once a holy man living at the top of a mountain. This man was so holy that even the birds would pay homage to him. Each day they would gather small pieces of bread and bring them so that he may eat. One day just by chance, this holy man became enlightened. From that moment onwards, the birds stopped coming.

Our purpose, through the practice of Vipassana and Loving Kindness meditation, is not to be holy or special, rather it is to be ordinary. To live in a simple way in the world, working, playing, spending time with our family and friends, and not deluding ourselves as being someone who is different.

We do what we do because we are what we are. Not special, not different, but simply in harmony with our heart. Not the intellectual or emotional heart of course, but our real heart. Our spiritual heart.

Once we begin this journey of spiritual purity the world ceases to hold any real attraction for us. It can no longer interest us in the way it used to do. As soon as we have discovered the flaw in that particular way of living, how can we ever fully go back to it? To continually seek happiness outside ourselves, in other people, in possessions or in the idea of simply 'having fun', and being entertained, becomes empty and so naturally, without any real effort, we turn our back on that way of living.

It is not that we begin to hate it, it is only that we understand its nature, and its nature is to be empty. However, no matter what we do, we cannot completely escape this world. Even if we no longer agree with its ways, it is still the place where we live. It is still our home. Now we need to learn how to live in the world, but no longer be a part of it.

But what does this mean?

How can we live in the world without being a part of it?

Many years ago I was faced with a spiritual crisis. I had done what most people in our society do, which was to fall in love, get married, set up home and begin to accumulate around me all the trappings of that kind of life. For two years, my wife and myself worked hard gathering every type of modern convenience. A washing machine, a video recorder, a hi-fi system, a television set, in fact, many television sets, one for every room, and so on and so on. We had a house filled with material possessions, but there was always something else to get. Always one more thing to add to our list of requirements needed to make us happy.
One day, I awoke with a start and felt myself to be completely trapped!
It seemed as though I was being suffocated in this house of material possessions and the strong, almost overwhelming desire to throw everything out descended upon me. Of course, my wife did not feel the same way, and told me that if we just had one more thing, a new car or another television set, I would feel better. It didn't work!
I could always justify my feelings of resentment to this material way of living when I would reflect upon my spiritual heroes. The Buddha had renounced everything for his enlightenment and had spent the six years prior to it as a wandering mendicant. Jesus was another homeless wanderer

and Gandhi was pleased to live with very little. These were the people I admired. Why couldn't I be like them? Free from the trap of possessions.
These feelings worried me for many months until finally, I attended another intensive Vipassana retreat with my own teacher. In a private interview, I told him exactly what was happening within me, and how I had a strong desire to throw everything out, or at least give them away and so free myself from the trap of material possessions. I wanted to live without them.
My teacher listened patiently and then simply smiled and said gently, "ah Michael, now you must learn to live with them."

In that moment I understood.

The problem was not with the objects, it was my resentment towards them. The trap was only in my own mind. I had sprung it myself and being unaware, had jumped in with both feet.
Objects are not dangerous, it is only our attachment to them that causes the problems. So the teaching is 'watch the attachment.'

When there is no attachment, everything can be used, enjoyed and let go of. This is true freedom. Living in the world and yet not being part of the world. There is no need to renounce anything.
We are trapped forever by the things we renounce, like the priest who is always talking about sex, or the prostitute who is always talking about God.

We do not have to ordain as monks or nuns, or reside in a cave as a hermit to live a spiritual life. We can live comfortably in the world and we can continue our practice. It is ourselves we have to watch, not the things outside us.

Everything is arising in our mind. All our pain, all our sorrow, all our attachment and all our suffering begins here. And this is where these conditions can end. In the mind.

So, look at yourself. Without judgment, without condemnation, without blame. See where your problems and difficulties really begin. Not in the world, but only in the mind. With this understanding, we can live in peace with everything as we no longer attempt to create certain special conditions for spiritual growth, but use everything that is presented to us.

Enjoy, what can be enjoyed, and let go.
Endure what has to be endured, and let go.

This is how we can all set ourselves free, not from the traps of the world, they are only imaginary anyway, but from the trap of our own mind.

Watch the attachment, because whatever we are attached to will hurt as, no matter how noble, no matter how moral, no matter how spiritual.

Watch the attachment and let go.

Liberation means freedom and freedom is always within us, just watch the attachment.

6 - Living in the past

*'There is no part of our being
that is not in a continual process of change
and that which we call 'self', is itself,
only a process of becoming
that never becomes anything.'*

A man went to a psychiatrist and exclaimed, "I'm Napoleon!" The psychiatrist replied, "you can't be Napoleon, he comes here on Wednesdays."

There is a great interest in past lives. So many people are concerned with finding out who they used to be that a whole industry has been established to cater to this demand. It seems obvious of course, but everyone wants to have been somebody famous, Napoleon, Queen Victoria, Alexander the great. No one is interested in discovering that they were just a poor homeless beggar living on the steps of a temple somewhere in Asia two hundred years ago. We need to feel that at least a past life had some glamour or point to it.

A student of mine once told me that he had been a disciple of the Buddha in a previous life. He had apparently discovered this with the use of a pendulum. By asking questions and spelling out words with the letters it pointed to, he was able to discover things about his past lives.
In this life, he was an ordinary working man, holding down a job in a factory and living with his family. So I pointed this out.
"You used to be a disciple of the Buddha, living the homeless life and seeking enlightenment, but now you are married

and work in a factory. Are you sure you're going in the right direction?"

Another student of mine told me that she once had afternoon tea with a man who revealed to her that in his past lives he had been William Shakespeare, Lord Horatio Nelson and T. S. Eliot. Now, that's fairly impressive, to have been not one, but three of the greatest figures in English history. And of course it does make a good opening to any conversation. "Hello, I'm Bob, I used to be Shakespeare."

In true Dhamma training, past lives mean nothing.

Our intention is to not only understand the mind and body as they really are, but to live in the present moment. When awareness of the present moment is fully established, there is no more past and no more future. We abide peacefully here and now with correct understanding. This understanding we call wisdom. It is not a belief. It is not a fanciful idea. It is not delusion. It is knowing, established in a direct and impartial understanding of our own human reality. It is the truth.
When we understand the mind through a peaceful and loving investigation we do not become entangled in its endless thoughts, ideas and fantasies. Then and only then can we know our own reality. We can experience directly our true nature.

No-one was ever born, and no-one will ever die.

As long as we have delusion however, it will always appear to be other than this. We will attach to the notion that we were somebody in the past and that we will be somebody in the future. This is how delusion manifests, as attachment and belief in the existence of 'self'. Something separate from what we feel we are. Something eternal and unchanging. Something that is what we 'really are'.

When we have clear understanding we will know for ourselves that there is no real or permanent 'self'. There is no part of our being that is not in a continual process of change and that which we call 'self', is itself only a process of becoming that never becomes anything.
We will recognise the mind for what it is, a never ending stream of thoughts, moods, feelings and emotions, always moving and always changing. From a beginningless beginning to an endless end.
Within this stream of change there is nothing to experience that we can call a real or an abiding 'self'. There is no 'you' that can be reborn.
There was no 'me' in the past and there will be no 'me' in the future.
When we impartially examine the concept of 'I', 'me', 'mine', and 'my', culminating in the belief of self in this present moment, we will see that it doesn't actually exist as something real. It is just an idea. It's just a convenient way of labelling a process of change that cannot be contained or defined in any way other than as a concept.
And concepts are not reality. They are not the truth. They are only labels we place on the truth. So what is there to be reborn?
The mind stream flows on and on, unhindered by the arising and cessation of the physical realm and so, using conventional language, we can talk about rebirth or reincarnation.
However, we must not become confused by the terms. There is no 'you' to be reborn, only the unrestricted and impartial movement of mind. Not me, not mine, not what I am. Only

the continuing process of mind.

When the Buddha was asked about karmic memory, the ability to remember past lives, he said that 'Even if you could remember one hundred thousand lives in great detail, none of those existences is 'you'.

It is only mind.
And so now consider, even if you were able to know conclusively that you were Lord Horatio Nelson in a past life. What does that mean to you now?
It is just a memory. Just like you remember waking up this morning and going to the bathroom. Above that it has no value. In this life, you are you with all your pain, unhappiness and delusion. Being Lord Nelson in a past life does not help you at all.

So let go of peripheral spirituality.
These days, encouraged by the so-called New Age, so much time and effort is spent in things of no consequence. Things that do not lead to the ending of suffering, and the experience of joy. Things that in fact, only encourage the cultivation and development of ego.
Past life, next life. It all means nothing. Only this life has value, because in this life you can do something. You can end your suffering.

When understanding arises, these types of questions fall away. They have no value.

Vipassana is a very special practice. Although we can say that all meditation is beneficial, other practices are only good as far as they go. If a particular type of meditation has the effect

of relaxing us and relieving stress and succeeds in that, then it has value. However, that value is relative. If the practice is missed even for a few days, the stress levels build up again and we are back to where we started.
No wisdom has been developed and no advantage gained.
It is like working in a garden. If you're a gardener you will know that to simply cut the heads off weeds whilst you are mowing the lawn will not prevent them from growing again. A few days later they are back again as strong as ever. To eradicate weeds permanently we have to dig them up. From the roots!

This is the function of the meditation practice known as Vipassana. No other practice will do this. To not only eradicate the symptoms of a mind no longer in harmony with itself, but to actually undermine the causes of those symptoms. Only this practice leads to wisdom. To knowing clearly beyond belief and ideas, the real nature of our existence, and so affect the way we live in the world.
We change the way we perceive the world because we change the way we perceive ourselves.

This is such a beautiful practice, beyond religion, beyond belief, beyond speculation. Dealing directly with the causes of our unhappiness and developing a lifestyle that transcends our usual limitations and restrictions. Finding ourselves in a position whereby, not only do we benefit, but ultimately all beings benefit.
When one more person turns to the practice of Vipassana and Loving Kindness meditation, the whole world benefits, because there is one more person living with wisdom and love, and one less person living from greed, hatred and delusion.

This is the joy and beauty of Vipassana, the realisation of the truth.

7 - Loving Awareness

'If the mind is not ours, why should we fight with it?'

At one time a young man went to a master and complained about his life.

"I have always had everything I wanted," he said, "and yet my life seems to be so empty. I am never able to stay with anything for very long and so I drift from one thing to the next. Now I even consider spiritual training to give my life some meaning, but I know, based on my past that I will eventually give it up and move on to something else. I have come to ask you for help."

The master thought for a moment and then replied, "I can help you if you truly wish it, but I must ask you one question. Is there anything in your life that you have been particularly good at?"

"Why yes," exclaimed the young man, " I was always good at chess."

"Excellent," cried the master, and immediately called for a monk to bring a chessboard, chess pieces and a sword.

"Now," said the master as the monk set up the chess pieces, "you two will play a game together. If my monk loses, I will cut off his head. If you lose, I will cut off yours. These are the only rules. Please begin."

The young man and the monk looked into the eyes of the Master and saw that he was deadly serious. It was to be a game to the death.

The game began and the monk was good. He made several skilful moves and soon took the advantage. But the young man was also good. He countered and the deadly game continued.

Then it happened. The monk made a mistake. The young man saw it at once and realised that the game was his for the taking. Three more moves and it would be checkmate. He would not only win the game but also his life. In his excitement and relief he glanced up at his opponent, and in a moment of clarity that took his breath away, saw:

Here was a man whose life has meaning and purpose. Even gazing into the eyes of imminent death, his face was serene and calm. If one of them had to die it should not be this man. The young man did not take advantage of the monks mistake but made a subtle move to put the game in the hands of his opponent. The game continued, the young man giving away more and more pieces until suddenly, the master gave a great shout and knocked over the board.

"There is no winner and no loser here today," he announced, "you have both played well."

He dismissed the monk and turned to the young man.

"You said that your life had no meaning, but today it was clear to me that it has far greater meaning than you think. You played the game with awareness, looking to take the advantage and so to win, but when you realised the consequences of winning, your heart was filled with love for a fellow human being, and you deliberately began to lose. If you can live your life with these two qualities of love and awareness, you have no need to wonder about giving it meaning."

The young man understood and smiled. He stayed with the master, surrendering himself to the two qualities of love and awareness, until he became a master himself.

Vipassana means awareness. It means to see things as they really are.

Awareness is the ground state for spiritual development. For knowing the truth. It is the state of non judgement and of simply seeing.
Through the cultivation of awareness, we begin to understand and know the mind for what it is, not 'me', not 'mine', not what 'I am', and so live peacefully with it.
If the mind is not 'ours', why should we fight with it?

Thoughts, moods, feelings and emotions arise and pass away in an endless succession. They never ask our permission or consent to visit us, nor do they ask our permission or consent to leave. They just come and go according to their nature.
Even if we make a decision not to experience a particular mental state, it makes no difference, it comes anyway. And if we decide that we would like other mental states to stay with us forever, that too makes no difference. They pass away.
This is the nature of the mind.
Whatever arises passes away.

If we want to end the struggle with life and find real and lasting happiness, we have to accept and live peacefully with the true nature of this mind. We have to accept it as it is. A never ending stream of thoughts, moods, feelings and emotions arising and passing away. Not 'me', not 'mine', not what 'I am'. If we cannot accept and harmonise with the mind as it is, we will suffer. It is that simple.

Our purpose in cultivating awareness is to know through our own direct experience, beyond books, beyond scripture and beyond the words of the master, the reality of this mind we foolishly think we own, call 'ours' and so take responsibility for.
Once we know the real nature of the mind, we will be able

to live peacefully with it. It will no longer have the power to take us on the emotional roller coaster ride we usually call life. No longer struggling when it presents unpleasant mental states to us, and no longer grasping at the pleasant ones. We will be in harmony with the mind. With life itself.

You are not your anger. You are not your fear. You are not your doubt.

There is anger. There is fear. There is doubt.

But these are not what you are. They are mind states that simply arise and pass away and in all cases, they only have the power that you give them. Once you identify with them, you become them.

You are not the anger, but you become it.
You are not the fear, but you become it.
You are not the doubt, but you become it.

The mind is not what you are, it is only that which you become.

Through simple awareness practice we can know the mind as it really is, and in that knowing be free from its influence. This is the power of the meditation practice, traditionally called Satipatthana, but now more popularly known as Vipassana.

However, if awareness is the ground state for spiritual development, love is the ground state for awareness.
In spiritual terms love means to be unconditionally accepting of ourselves, others and the situation we find ourselves in.

It means not to judge from our own personal perspective of how things should be, but gives the space for everything to be exactly as it is. This of course includes other beings, even if we don't like them, even if we don't approve of them or their conduct, even if they try to hurt us.
With love, we allow everything to be exactly as it is. We give ourselves permission to accept this life as it unfolds. On the personal, interpersonal and universal levels.

If we cannot control the mind that we call 'ours', how can we control anything else?

Everything is acting in accordance with its nature. With awareness we can see this. With love, we can allow it.

From the position of loving awareness, we will be able to act fully and freely in the world. Not from self-interest. Not from preconceived ideas. Not from personal demands that everyone and everything be exactly as we think they should be, but from freedom, from confidence and from truth.
When we live with loving awareness, we will see the limitless potential that life truly offers. We will flow with the mind and consequently, with the whole of life.

This is freedom. This is liberation. This is loving awareness.

Not This

8 - Who will wash the dishes?

'Whatever you think you are, you are not.'

A young man went to his girlfriend's house for a meal. When the meal was finished, his girlfriend excused herself and went to see another friend for an hour. Whilst she was away, the boyfriend made himself busy and washed, dried and put away all the dishes.
When the girlfriend returned the young man smiled at her and said, "I have washed all the dishes for you."
The girlfriend smiled back and replied, "Thank you, but it's not my job."

Our culture, as with all cultures in the world, believes in and supports conditioning and role-playing. It is the practice of taking our identity from what we do, rather than what we are, and it begins in our infancy, when we are given rigid guidelines of behaviour and conduct by our parents, our educational system and the rest of society in general. If we are a boy, one set of conditions apply. If we are a girl, another set applies. And of course, because we don't know any differently, we accept the identity we are given, and even if we don't like it we find great support in it. It tells us who and what we are and how we should be.

Two babies were lying next to each other in the maternity home.
"Are you a boy or a girl? asked one.
"I don't know," came the answer, "how about you?"
"Oh, I'm a boy," the first baby replied.
"How do you know?" the other continued.

The first baby lifted the sheets and pointed down, "look," he said, "blue booties."

Dhamma means truth. It is a Buddhist word that means, 'that which is behind the appearance of things'. The whole purpose of Dhamma training is to see behind the illusoriness of life, and having seen and experienced it for ourselves, go beyond it's outward manifestation. It is not a system of belief or blind faith. The Dhamma master does not want you to believe how things are. They want you to know. For yourself and by yourself.

Belief is not the truth. Believe is what we cultivate when we don't know the truth. And belief, any belief, is just more conditioning. It is simply more clinging to delusion. Even if what we believe is true, until we discover that truth for ourselves, we still don't know.
We spend the whole of our life supporting and then reaffirming our apparent identity, so it often comes as a great shock when the Dhamma master tells the student, 'Whatever you think you are, you are not.'

There is nothing that you really are nor have to be.

One great teacher told a student one day, 'You are not a man, you are not a woman.' The student was astounded.
He walked away muttering, 'I am a man, I am a man'.

But 'man' only exists in relationship to 'woman'. 'Big', only exists in relationship to 'small'. 'High', only exists in relationship to 'low'. 'Fat', only exists in relationship to 'thin'. 'Good', only exists in relationship to 'bad'.
When you stand at the sink by yourself washing the dishes,

are you a man or woman? Are you tall or short? Are you attractive or plain?
There is simply a being engaged in an activity. Not man, not woman. Not tall, not short. Not attractive, not plain. Not good, not bad.

In the world it is just the same.
Secretary is not what you are, it is something that you do. Parent is not what you are, it is something that you do. Bus driver is not what you are, it is something that you do.
These roles are not you, they are like hats that you wear on different occasions. You are not the hat, you are only the being wearing it.
But when we are trapped by a conditioning, and role-playing, we feel it is our job to tidy the house, wash the dishes, do the ironing, or put up shelves, fix the car and mend the fuse. We even defend our position when we say, 'well, if I don't do it, who will?'

But the truth says something different.

It is not your job to do anything.
It is not a cosmic or universal law that says certain people have to do one thing in life, whilst others have to do something else. These are just roles we assume. It is only our conditioning.

If you want to wash the dishes, wash them, but don't think it's your job. If you want to clean the house, clean it but don't think it's your job. If you want to fix the car, fix it, but don't think it's your job. If you want to put up shelves, put them up but don't think it's your job.

Not This

Do it because you want to do it, and take pleasure in it. Do it because you have chosen to do it. Do it because it is what you want to do. Do it with love.

And if you don't want to do these things, don't do them!

But remember, none of us lives in isolation. Everything we do is affecting everyone and everything else, so to suddenly change the habit of a lifetime or a role that you have played for a long time will have an effect on the people around you. So be prepared, but be resolute.

And when the sink is piled high with dirty dishes, because no one else has seen the need to wash them and you, out of habit, cannot stand the sight or inconvenience of them dirty anymore, begin to wash them, remember, you are doing this for you, and because you're doing it for you, do it with love.

It's not your job, but you have chosen to do it.

So do it for you, because it's how you like things to be done.
Do it with love, because you're doing it for yourself.
Do it without resentment, because if it's not your job, it's no one else's either!

Dhamma tells us that there is nothing that we really are nor have to be.
We are not the things that we do, we are only the being that does them and ultimately we are doing them for ourselves.
So relax, smile and be happy. This is your life - enjoy.

9 - Open your own treasure house

*'There is no truth outside yourself,
and nowhere to find it,
other than within yourself.'*

At one time Daiju visited the master Baso in China.
Baso asked, "What do you seek?" "Enlightenment," replied Daiju.
"You have your own treasure house, why do you seek outside?" asked Baso.
Daiju inquired, "Where is my treasure house?"
Baso answered, "What you're asking for is contained within your own treasure house." Daiju was enlightened.
From then on he urged his own disciples to open their own treasure house and use those treasures.

There is a common misunderstanding in spiritual practice that we do what we do to acquire some special qualities and that there is something to get from outside ourselves. Something that we don't already have. Something that will make our life perfect.
It is the lottery syndrome. We feel that if only we could win a large amount of money in the national lottery, then all our problems would end. Our life would become happier because all our reasons for worry and concern would be removed. Certainly, with correct planning, we would never have to think about paying the gas or electricity bills again, we would always have enough to eat, and somewhere comfortable to stay. Our anxieties for the future would diminish to the point of disappearance. From the position of being well provided for, our life would seem to be perfect. Actually, it is the

dream of most people anywhere in the world to win or inherit a large sum of money so that the threat of unhappiness can be removed from their horizon.
This is the lottery syndrome, that there is something waiting for us in the future that can be acquired and our permanent and lasting happiness realised.
Without understanding, it is the same in the spiritual life.

It is an idea that what we are doing now is actually a preparation for something in the future. We meditate now, not for what we can realise now, but for some realisation in the future. We are doing what we are doing, because someday it will all come right and we will find real and lasting happiness. We will have developed the qualities of peace, calm and equanimity at the expense of anger, fear and doubt. These are the things we feel we have to acquire and in order to get them we may have to travel to India, or Tibet, or China, or Japan, or any other exotic place and find an enlightened teacher, who can give them to us. We have to go to a special place, a place where the teaching is.
Daiju, the seeker in the story, however was stopped dead in his tracks. He had travelled from Japan to China to sit at the feet of a master. Travelling in those days was no easy matter, long difficult sea journeys and rough treks overland, perhaps lasting many weeks or months, to find a teacher living in a remote part of the country. Even then, there would be no certainty that the teacher would be there or even if he would accept disciples. To find a teacher in those days took determination and resolution. There were no books, no internet and no weekend seminars. The disciple had to be determined and resolute and make the effort for himself. Daiju was like this and so made the difficult journey to find the famous teacher.

Not This

"What do you want?" asked the master.
He is asking Daiju why he has come. Why he has made a long and difficult journey to sit at the feet of an old man. What is it that he thinks will happen?
"I want enlightenment," replied Daiju.
I want the special qualities that will make my life worthwhile. I want to know why I was born and why I must die. I want to know the reason for things being the way they are. But most of all I want certainty. I want to be able to live and know that I'm not wasting my life.
This was the answer of Daiju, neatly contained in the phrase, 'I want enlightenment'.
Enlightenment is the magical quality that will ensure happiness. Perfect peace of mind. But his understanding was wrong. It was not enlightenment he wanted. He didn't know what enlightenment was. Until we experience it for ourselves, we cannot know. We can only form views and opinions around it.
He wanted security. He wanted peace. He wanted to win the lottery.
However, as he kneels at the feet of Baso, one of China's most famous and most respected masters, his heart opens. In that moment his mind clears of all his long-held views and opinions as to what enlightenment is, and he experiences a peacefulness never before encountered. He waits without waiting. Simply being present, and into that now receptive mind, the master's voice rings.
"You have your own treasure house, why do you seek outside."

There is a moment of struggle. The simplicity of the masters teaching is astounding.
He asks, "Where is my treasure house?"

Baso answers with a smile, "What you're asking for is contained within your own treasure house."

There is no truth outside yourself and no place to find it other than within yourself. Enlightenment is not some special quality we need to acquire, rather it is the ordinary quality we already have. The Buddha did not get enlightenment, he realised it! The things that you believe to be obstacles to enlightenment are in fact the very things that will lead you to it.

Greed, anger, fear, doubt, confusion are natural conditions of mind, common to all human beings. Learn to see them for what they really are and they will lead you to the place where the mind is not continually repressing or indulging them, but able to live peacefully with them. Enlightenment lies in surrender. In giving up picking and choosing between the pleasant and unpleasant and happily accepting all conditions as they arise and pass away in every moment. This is how we recognise the true nature of endless change.

Enlightenment begins with this mind body complex. One cannot realise it for another, nor can one pass it on to another. It is completely impersonal in this sense, although once experienced it is a blessing to the whole of mankind.

This is how Daiju understood the masters teaching, and in that moment of pure understanding, enlightenment arose. No more needed to be done. There was nothing left to accomplish.

This is the treasure house, we all have to open.

This story happened many years ago, but in reality, nothing has changed.

As spiritual seekers, we continually look outside ourselves

for those special qualities we believe to be enlightenment. Those feelings of peace and contentment. In fact, we generally use the expression 'good meditation', to indicate that the mind has been calm and peaceful and that the time has passed quickly and without effort. If however, we have experienced feelings of desire or restlessness or any painful sensations in the body, we will say something else. That was definitely not a 'good meditation'.

As long as we associate a feeling of 'getting high' on peacefulness with our meditation practice we are still a long way from truth.

The purpose of Dhamma practice in general and Vipassana training in particular, is to see the mind as it is in this moment, and not try to make it any particular way. To learn to let go of our desire to change everything so that it is always perfect for us and be at peace with things as they are. With this attitude we can know the truth for ourselves and everything in the mind body complex can be used as a treasure. By using those treasures and taking advantage of their qualities, we can realise enlightenment for ourselves.

No-one can do this for us. Our practice is personal to us because our mind is personal to us.

The world that we experience is the one that we create for ourselves, moment after moment. Even the master can't help very much. Masters can only point the way, it is ourselves that must do the work.

It is not possible to say how difficult it is to be born as a human being, but according to Buddhist teachings, it is only human beings that have the capacity to realise enlightenment. Our life then, is an opportunity not to be missed.

We all take our life for granted, thinking that it will last for ever, that things will just go on and on, never realising that the very nature of life is to be uncertain. In actual fact, we never know from one moment to the next what can happen. Even when we hear of accidents or tragedies befalling others, we never really believe that the same thing can happen to us. The truth is, we just don't know, and because of this very reason we cannot assume that time or destiny is on our side. Part of spiritual training is to recognise this fundamental reality, and then do something about it. And what we have to do is practice.

Practice is not something special in life. Practice is life.

There is no separation between our ordinary life, the things we do, the places we go to, the people we spend our time with and our spiritual practice. In the end, it is always the same thing, because the objects of our practice, the things we need to examine and investigate are always with us. They are mind and body.
No more is needed, we don't need to wear special clothes, have our hair a certain way, cover our heads or grow beards. We don't need to travel to remote monasteries high in the Himalayas or trudge around various exotic countries looking for teachers or masters. Here we already have everything we need. Mind and body. It is enough.
The only skill we need to develop is how to use them in the right way. A way that is beneficial to ourselves and others. It doesn't matter where we are or what we are doing, when our mind is centred and in balance and we are in a position to be aware of the arising and cessation of our desires and aversions. To observe our habitual fear based reactions to control everyone and everything so that they will always be perfect for us.

This is our practice, and this is our treasure house!

The very things we fight with, the very things we struggle against and try to change become the objects of our attention. From these we learn the impermanent nature of all phenomena. When we understand this, we are free. These are the teachers and these are our treasures. Enlightenment is not in some special time or place, it is right here with us, right now. All we have to do is turn to it. To be it.
It is not about creating special qualities and gaining something magical. It is about allowing the beautiful qualities that we already have to come forth, and not permit ego and conceit to stand in their way.

And so I don't say develop love, I say be loving.
I don't say develop compassion, I say be compassionate.
I don't say develop wisdom, I say be wise.

Everything you want, you already have. There is nothing to get, only that which can be realised. Treasures are rare and precious. You, yourselves are treasure houses filled with the most wonderful things. Open your own treasure house and use those treasures.

Be free - now.

10 - Insight and belief

'Without the practice of Vipassana meditation, even this teaching becomes a religion.'

There was once a master who overheard a group of monks discussing the Buddha's teaching. As he listened, he became curious as to their level of understanding and decided to question them.
"There is a big stone," he said pointing into the distance, "do you consider it to be inside or outside your mind?"
One monk replied, "from the Buddhist viewpoint, everything is an objectification of mind, so I would say the stone is definitely inside my mind."
"Then your head must feel very heavy indeed, if you are carrying around a stone such as that," said the master.

One thing has become very clear to me in the years that I have been presenting the teachings of Dhamma, and that is people's reaction to it. Many say of course, that they come to meditate, but more so, to hear me talk, tell some stories and explain the teaching. In fact, I have been asked if it is possible just to practice the teachings without having to sit in meditation at all?
This is a very good question, and worthy of consideration.

One of the guiding forces in society is religion. Usually this is the mass acceptance of a spiritual teaching that has come from the distant past. However, to be a part of this acceptance gives one a place in society and a structure to one's life, with obligations and duties, rites and rituals. Very often, the reason for these things will have been long forgotten, but now it is tradition. It is the way things have always been done.

At one time in India there was a guru. When he would sit down to meditate in the evening, the ashram cat would enter the meditation hall and distract the followers, so the guru ordered that the cat be tied to a post during these times.
After the guru had died, the cat continued to be tied to the post during the evening meditation. Eventually the cat itself died and another cat was brought to the ashram, so it too could be tied to the post during the evening meditation.
Hundreds of years later, great and respected scholars would write long intellectual treaties on the spiritual significance of tying a cat to a post during the evening meditation.

It is true that religion really outlines the highest spiritual ideals of man and Christianity is a perfect example of this.
To all spiritual seekers, Jesus and his teachings are the manifestation of love, compassion and forgiveness. However, Christianity functions as a system of belief and faith. Christian people are taught to accept the words of the Bible as true, and not question the dogma of the Church. They are told to pray and put their faith in God, even when their faith is severely tested. At this time, they are told to accept that God works in mysterious ways, 'his wonders to perform', and that we cannot begin to understand his divine logic.
However, God has dictated certain ways that we should live, and certainly as in the case of Christianity, these ways are of the highest order. But as with all religions, it is possessive. Jesus was the son of God and it is only through faith and belief in him that salvation can be attained. No other course will do.
Jesus tells us wisely to 'turn the other cheek'. Whenever we are abused, either physically or verbally, we are not to take

offence or repay like with like, but to 'turn the other cheek'. To continually offer love, compassion and forgiveness to all the beings that offend us. Jesus also tells us to love our enemies. That we should live in peace and harmony with all beings, even if those beings are actively trying to harm us.
These are beautiful teachings and the mark of a true spiritual master is the ability to manifest these teachings spontaneously, moment after moment, in their ordinary life.

But for those who are not masters, what can they do?
Is it really possible to develop the high mindedness necessary to live in such a way?

This is the failing point for all theistic religions. They point to a perfectly pure life, but offer no clear practice as to how to attain it.

All religions have within them factions that follow specific spiritual traditions, such as the Sufis in the Islamic faith, the desert fathers of the Christians, the Indian Tantric and yoga systems and of course, the Vipassana and other awareness meditation systems of Buddhism.
These are established upon the original teachings of the founder and all involve self investigation and realisation. The turning away from the world of the ego and the surrender into the world of wisdom, love and compassion.
However, for most of the world's population, these traditions are buried and the way to lead a spiritual lifestyle is to believe in something.

This level of spirituality creates all kinds of problems for us. Without training and guidance its ideals are almost impossible to live up to and yet threatens punishment if we fail. It creates a situation of conflict within us as we try to allow God's will to be done without ever fully understanding exactly what that will is.

If we truly want to understand God's will we have to do something very special. We have to stop listening to the continual chatter of ego, that part of us that can always justify and rationalise every deed we perform, no matter how horrendous. We have to allow the mind to find its point of balance. This is attained through the silent practice of meditation.

At one time Mother Theresa of Calcutta was interviewed by a young journalist.
"Do you still pray," asked the journalist.
"Yes, I pray every day," said Mother Theresa.
"What do you say?" asked the journalist.
"I don't say anything," said Mother Teresa, "I listen."
"And what does God say?" continued the journalist.
"He doesn't say anything," replied Mother Teresa, "He listens."

My own spiritual background is in the Buddhist practice of Vipassana and Loving Kindness (Metta Bhavana) meditation, and so I often quote the Buddha and his teaching to emphasise different aspects of development. But my intention is only to illustrate a point. It is never to try and convert students to a new system of belief. Vipassana does not operate in this way. Even though it is the direct teaching of the Buddha, it is not Buddhist. It is not belief or blind faith. It is a way of realising the truth for ourselves.

To progress along the spiritual path, to free ourselves from the bonds of wrong thought and delusion, we have to go beyond belief. We have to experience the truth for ourselves.

To say, 'I used to believe in God, but now I believe in Allah', doesn't help anyone. It's just more of the same. More belief and ultimately more suffering.

The Buddhist path as a system for enlightenment is deep and profound, but the understanding and subsequent teaching of the Buddha came directly from his meditation. If we want to understand his teaching at it's deepest level, we have to return to that place. The place of meditation. The silent mind. The Buddhist scriptures are said to be thirteen times larger than the Bible, but you could read it all, every word and still not know what the Buddha taught. Knowing comes from meditation. Understanding, true understanding that spontaneously manifests in every moment of our life, comes only through the process of investigation into the very cause of our suffering and discontent. This process of investigation traditionally called Satipatthana, we now call Vipassana. Without the practice of Vipassana even this teaching becomes a religion. Another system of belief.
You begin to accept what I say, not because through investigation, you find it to be true but simply because I say it. If this begins to happen, there will be real difficulties for you.

I tell you to 'let go', of your desire to control and manipulate everything. I explain how we all suffer from this particular human tendency and outline the problems that arise when we simply follow our impulses. As you hear these words you feel that you begin to understand, after all, the truth is not a secret, it is only the obvious. But your understanding comes from the rational mind and the intellect. You feel that what I say is true, and perhaps in a moment of inspiration you actually raise the intention to no longer follow the seemingly natural desire to control everyone and everything around you.

But how do we actually do that? How do any of us break the habits of a lifetime?

It is only meditation, that will do this, because only meditation will illuminate that place in the mind were all our desires and natural tendencies begin. Once we know their place of origin, we are in a position to do something about them. Namely, let them go. Stop attaching to them. Stop grasping them in the belief that they are really what we are, and recognise their true nature. Impermanent movements of mind, not 'me', not 'mine', not what 'I am'.

Let them go. Let them all go.

Slowly, slowly we can allow the reservoir of ego and conceit to empty and permit the pure mind to manifest. There is no difference between the meditation and the teachings. They are like two hands that wash each other, cleansing each other and resulting in the purity that is wisdom.

Wisdom is the result of true spiritual practice. Not blind faith and not belief.

Without wisdom, based in our own direct experience of truth, we are like the monk in the story. He knows what the teaching says, but not from personal realisation. Only from books and the words of others. Without direct experience of the truth, no matter how powerful the words are, they are always someone else's and we simply carry them around with us.

Like a great big stone in our head.

11 - Why do we do this?

'From here we can only go forward, never back.'

(Taken from an evening Dhamma talk during an intensive Vipassana retreat at the International Meditation Centre, Budh Gaya, India. January 1993.)

There is a Zen koan that asks, 'In such a wide world, why do we wear the ceremonial robes and answer the call of a bell?'

There are many different types of meditation, ranging from the simple transcendental style of Maharishi Mahesh Yogi, to the deepest trance like states taught by other Indian gurus. You can make your own choice.
Even the Buddha himself taught forty different types of meditation, according to what was suitable for the disciple at the time.

All these techniques have different aims and goals, however there is only one aim and goal we are interested in here. The development of spiritual insight.
I use the term 'spiritual insight', so as not to confuse the objective of our time together with some sort of deep academic or intellectual understanding. Our aim is not to understand what we experience from an intellectual perspective, but to know directly the process of mind and body.
The purpose of spiritual practice is the development of insight. Actually, there is no value to practice, other than this. Insight is something special. It is something different from the usual things we seek. Insight means to see clearly and without any form of attachment or ideas, beliefs, views and

opinions, the reality of our own existence. It means to know the truth.

In one intensive retreat in India some years ago we had a large group of American psychologists. They all sat well together and were good students. At the end of the retreat all of them came to see me individually to say goodbye and thank you. It was during our last moments together that almost all of them told me the same thing, which was that they now thought that everyone who wants to be a practicing psychologist should sit at least one, ten day intensive Vipassana retreat. When I asked them why they now thought this, they replied, 'because there is a difference between knowing about the mind, and knowing the mind directly.'

Vipassana is knowing the mind directly.

When true insight arises there is no distinction between the knower and the known. There is only the knowing. Insight is the knowing.
Here we practice Vipassana meditation in the style of bare attention, but we should understand that this is only a particular style of Vipassana. There are many styles, this is just one. We must not confuse style with The Path. A practice of meditation is something that can help us on The Path, but it is not The Path itself. Do you understand?

We may have a practice, but we may not have The Path.

Many people get caught up in style and practice. Even teachers make claims that their system is the best and that others are inferior. It's just delusion and it's just salesmanship. In the spiritual life, we have to apply the practice that is appropriate to the situation.

We have to know our own practice and not become confused by the experience of others. What works for one may not work for another. As with all things spiritual we have to be open. In Vipassana meditation we focus our attention on the uncontrolled and impersonal movement of breath in the nostrils or abdomen. From this beginning, everything else follows naturally. The non-attached awareness of mind, no longer habitually selecting only the most interesting and desirable mental states, leads to a direct experience of ourselves. The experience of insight.

Other traditions have their own styles. All valid.

In Rinzai Zen, one of the systems used to cultivate insight is known as koan study.

This particular approach to insight was discovered by the master Rinzai when he found that his disciples had mind's that were so busy, so inquisitive, that they had a difficult time simply watching the breath. They loved to think. He found the solution. He would really give them something to think about! He devised a series of questions and statements that defy the logical, rational thinking mind. Understanding of the koan cannot be attained through the intellect, only through intuition. It cannot be answered, it can only be understood. The understanding is insight.

Some of the better-known koans are:

I am turning on the light where does the darkness go?

We all know the sound that two hands make when they clap together, but what is the sound of one hand clapping?

Show me your original face, the face you had before your mother and father were born.

The koan at the beginning of the talk is not so well-known but it is appropriate. It asks the question, 'why do we do this?'

The world is a big place, and from the moment we are born we spend all of our time and effort making that place as comfortable as possible. We do this of course, by a complete indulgence in the senses. Always looking for total satisfaction through the empowerment of the senses.
Take, for example, the eating of food. Food actually only has one function, and that is to sustain the body. Nothing else. However, throughout the world food is prepared to excite and stimulate not only the palate, but also the eye and the nose. It must smell good, look good and taste good, and each meal should be superior to the last. It should inspire curiosity and comparison. From its basic level of pure practicality, we have taken food, its preparation and service, not forgetting social etiquette, to an art form. Whether we realise it or not, we are always looking for the perfect meal.

This is true of all our sensory experiences.

To spend our time continually looking for perfection in the senses is not wrong, it's just pointless. Everything we do has to be - and can be - bettered.

Washing powders have been improved upon year after year ever since they first arrived on the market. Ingredients added, ingredients taken away. New chemical formulas, new biological formulas. Now, many many years later, you might believe that they are complete, everything needed for the perfect wash but wait, tomorrow or the next day, someone will offer a new and better powder to give the customer not only a perfect wash, but a new and enhanced lifestyle.

To be caught up in this way of life takes us only in one direction, round and round. Ever turning from moment to moment, lifetime to lifetime. This is the sensual world.
Not bad, but no good.
In every aspect of living we seek perfect fulfilment, and this way of thinking also applies to our mental states. Always looking for the new experience that will produce the perfect happiness. This feeling of satisfaction is how we understand, from a position of spiritual ignorance, the concept of self.

All of us are born with natural tendencies. Some of these dispositions are hard to identify as having any foundation in this lifetime. Many people are attracted to things that others find hard to accept. Like Tibetan butter tea.
This is a drink made with rancid butter, and served generously with dry bread at Tibetan monasteries. In Dharamsala in Northern India, I heard one young American enthusing about the merits of this particular beverage, whilst the rest of us who had sampled it, were not so enthusiastic!
We all have natural qualities, tendencies and interests that appear to come from nowhere. One young woman I know accompanied a friend one evening to a target rifle shooting club. For the next five years, she was the Lady Champion of that area. Natural ability.

For myself, I used to irritate and drive my father completely crazy with my interest in spiritual matters, even from a very early age. For me it was only a natural enquiry, for him it was very strange.

Each one of us here has a natural inclination towards a spiritual life. It is impossible to say where this inclination originated, but for all of us it manifests in the same way. The recognition that the world of the senses, emotions, feelings and all the things that we usually associate with being a 'normal person', is flawed. That no matter how much faith or confidence, we put into that world, it always leads back to this place. Sitting cross-legged on the floor in a Dhamma hall somewhere in the world.

There is nothing in the life of the senses, not one thing, that does not have this quality. This is how the sensual world teaches us, but so few recognise it as the teaching. For most it is the spur to further worldly pursuit. To increase the quality of the goal.

But for us, it's different.

We are now trapped in this life. Once we begin to train ourselves in the right way the trap was sprung and now we can never go back. Once we glimpsed the flaw in that particular system, we were caught. From here we can only go forward, never back. There is nothing to go back to.

On meditation retreats like this, we often find our minds wandering into fantasy, thinking about how wonderful it would be to give up all this pain and stiffness in our joints, to let go of our mental discomfort and take a long soak in a bath of hot, scented water and just relax. A real escape from suffering.

But I ask you, even if you did that, even if you left the discomfort and frustration of meditation behind you and luxuriated in a sweet smelling bath of perfumed water, easing the pain from your body and your mind, how long would it be before you are back here again?

How long before you are back, watching the breath in the nostrils and the sensations in the body?

The escape from pain is always temporary and no permanent or lasting satisfaction can be found. Not in food. Not in music. Not in the theatre. Not in television. Not in the movies. Not in relationships. Not in enjoyment. Not in the sensual world.

Not anywhere.

So, you come back here to face yourself. To seek the truth. To find the way.

This is what we have to do, you and I. We have no choice. For us living in the world offers no hope at all. Everything we were encouraged to establish our hopes and dreams upon to bring us lasting happiness has been revealed as insubstantial, empty. We must learn to transcend that world to go beyond and experience for ourselves the freedom that living a truly spiritual life offers.

The koan at the beginning asks, why do we do what we do? Why do we pursue this goal of spiritual liberation, when the world offers so many distractions and entertainments to please and stimulate us? The answer is simple:

Because our spiritual heart demands it!

12 - The purpose of meditation

*'Once we are born
we are all subject to the ravages of life.'*

There was once a monk who was being solely supported by one lady lay disciple.
Monks do not work and so have no means of livelihood. Because of this they need lay supporters, people who will provide them with food, shelter, clothing and medicine. In return for these services, the monk should dedicate himself to a life of spiritual pursuit. This is an unwritten agreement between the two. Also, it is the monks responsibility to perform any religious duties, such as blessings or teachings. It is a relationship of balance, one provides the spiritual support, whilst the other provides the material.
This lady had been supporting the monk for more than twenty years. Each day she had supplied food and drink to the small hut she had built especially for him in the mountains, but she never disturbed him. She was happy for him to continue his practice in isolation.
One day, however, she grew curious. After all those years of isolated practice she wanted to know for herself the depth of this man's spiritual understanding. She employed the services of a beautiful young woman of the town and asked her to test the monk by embracing him passionately and then suddenly asking, "what now?"
The beautiful young woman agreed and did as she was paid to do.
She threw herself at the monk and then asked in no uncertain terms just what he was going to do about it.
The monk replied somewhat poetically, "an old tree grows on

a cold rock in winter, nowhere is there any warmth."
The hired woman returned and reported what had been said. The lady supporter was furious.
"To think," she said, "I have been feeding him and looking after his needs for all these years. He showed no consideration for your desires, and no disposition to explain. He need not have responded with passion, but he could have at least shown some compassion."
With that, she went to the hut of the monk and burned it down.

There are people I know who like to do nothing more than meditate. I think some of them would spend a whole life on retreat, if they could. In fact, one person I know spends his life travelling from place to place in Asia, just to do retreats. Meditation practice is generally understood to be the cornerstone of spiritual development.

But retreats have to have a purpose. There has to be a point to them and a reason to make this effort. The have to have an effect on the way we live our life on a day-to-day basis, otherwise they are just an escape from the world. A running away from real life. To sit in meditation hour upon hour, day after day, week after week, month after month, is not the point. Whether understanding arises is the point, and that understanding by itself has little value, unless we can demonstrate it.

The monk in the story was an expert meditator. For twenty years he had sat in his hut developing his mind to the very highest levels and perhaps be able to understand the most subtle and profound truths. Maybe he had experienced deep insights into the nature of reality, who knows? But when he was approached by a lady in distress he was unable to help her. For his own part he was able to resist the powers of sexual desire, and not be drawn into that particular aspect of relationship, but the intention to help this lady understand what was happening within her did not arise. After all these years of practice the person he still places at the centre of his world is himself.

He was okay. An old tree on a cold rock. No warmth anywhere. No danger to himself, the fires of passion having long since died out, but more important than that, no compassion for anyone else.

A young woman went to her spiritual Master and said, "please excuse me, but I have fallen in love with you and now have the fantasy of us making love together."

The teacher smiled and said, "that's all right, it is not a problem that you feel this way. You can be in peace because I have enough discipline for both of us."

One of the main characteristics of progress in spiritual training is the arising of compassion, the recognition that everyone struggles with life. Externally, it may not seem that way as millionaires and other wealthy people seem on the surface, to have an easy time in life, living in comfort and style, whilst people at the lower end of the social scale have a difficult time, simply providing enough food for their family. It is easy to take an unsympathetic attitude towards the rich and give all our attention to the poor, but this is just the appearance of things.

As human beings each one of us without exception, is subject to the same conditions of life. Old age, sickness and finally death. Combined with this are all the fears, anxieties and worries that are simply part of taking life and living in the world. Once we are born, we are all subject to the ravages of life.

Modern medical science has improved our health expectations considerably, but it has not been able to eradicate the realities of old age, sickness and death from our horizon. The quality of a life may differ from person to person, but to die is cast for all of us.

The difference between the rich and the poor is that the rich suffer in comfort.

By Western standards the majority of people in India live at a low level of existence, but that doesn't mean they're unhappy. Of course, it doesn't mean they're happy either, it only shows that the world struggles with the realities of life from different perspectives. No need to hate the rich just because they are rich, no need to love the poor just because they are poor. Better to recognise that all beings meet with the same realities of life and develop compassion for all of them.

The purpose of spending long hours in meditation on retreat is to recognise that mental impulses come and go without end. It is not to get something, it is only to see something.

From this simple understanding we can know the mind directly and realise for ourselves that 'As it is for me, so it is for others'.

We will recognise that fear, anger, doubt, confusion, greed, conceit and every other mental state arises and passes way in our mind in exactly the same way as they arise and pass away in the mind of others. This understanding, this recognition of 'oneness', is called compassion.

We know intuitively that the mind of all human beings is exactly the same, and this is the source of suffering. Not the external conditions but the mind itself.

As we come to know this mind more and more, to truly understand its nature and so develop the ability to 'let go' and detach ourselves from the grip of our mental states, we will naturally feel the desire to help and to be of service to those still struggling through the delusion of life.

To lock ourselves away from the world for twenty years, may make us peaceful and happy, but in no way demonstrate spiritual progress.

However, to share the little we have discovered, by being of service to others and helping all the many beings that we share our life with, is a real demonstration of compassion.

13 - Seeing things as they really are

*'We put our faith in an idea of happiness
without understanding where real happiness lies.'*

A student came to a master and complained of an uncontrollable temper.
"That is something very strange you have there," said the master, "please show it to me."
"Right now I cannot," said the student.
"When can you show me?" asked the master.
"It always arises unexpectedly," answered the student.
"Then it cannot be your own true nature," concluded the master, "for if it was, you could show it to me at any time."

This is the nature of the mind. It comes and goes of its own accord. It never asks our permission or consent, it just arises and disappears by itself. Exactly when we think we have everything under control it lets us down, and we find ourselves reacting to a situation in the very way we had planned not to. Perhaps we resort to anger, or insults or some other tendency completely unworthy of us.
To be victims of the mind is the usual state for human beings. Just like the animal world.

If we make a comparison with the animal world, human beings would always hold themselves to be superior. After all, we plan, scheme, outline our lives and believe ourselves to be masters of our own destiny. This is true however, for only a very small number of people. Most people live their life completely at the mercy of their mental states.
Under these conditions, we may see the mind as the enemy,

something that will lift us to the heights of happiness, only to cast us down to the depths of despair at a moments notice. Without realising it, this is how we experience our life. Not in control, although sincerely believing that we are, and suffering the sad effects of such a great delusion. When anger arises in the mind, sometimes for reasons we are not even aware of, we react in a violent way. Slamming doors, using bad language, and generally acting in a manner unbefitting a superior being.

When animals experience a mental state they are completely overwhelmed by it and so become that thing. No rationalisation, no discussion, no awareness, only the action. A total immersion into the mental state experienced at that moment.

If we are cat owners and offer food to our cat, there is absolutely no point at all in expecting it to wait patiently whilst it is being prepared. The moment it senses the tin or packet being opened it wants the contents immediately!
Not sometime in the future. Not in the seven seconds it takes to walk across the kitchen floor, but now! Right now!
The moment that any animal experiences a mental state it completely becomes that thing. Human beings are the same. A little more restrained due to social conditioning, but nevertheless the same.

This apparently natural form of behaviour generally goes unnoticed until we begin to observe the mind in a very precise way. But for the most part, because it is considered usual and normal behaviour, we pay no attention. We do not realise that we are slaves of our mind.

The usual view is that to have strong feelings, to be passionate, to have deep emotions is the very essence of being alive. Of

being a vital human being.
Poets, songwriters and playwrights describe these powerful states of being, experiencing and illustrating them in such a way that very often all who read their words want to taste life like that. To feel totally alive through the effects of love and lust, and then to wish oneself to be dead, because of the opposite effects of pain and heartbreak. To be like this meant to be a fully alive human being.

Actually, to be like this means to be a victim.

To be like this means to find ourselves sitting astride a wild and unbroken stallion. It kicks and bucks and all we can do is hold on the best we can and wait until it slows down to walk. But as much as we may want to, we can't get off until the ride is finished!
And it is the stallion of the mind, who decides when that will be.

The Buddha, the meditation master of the aeon, has said that it is easier to tame a wild animal than to train your own mind. This is the absolute truth as any disciple of Vipassana will tell you.

Of course, we know that it is possible for the mind to be calm and peaceful. Sometimes, after a hard sporting activity and we have showered and changed and are sitting in the bar enjoying a nice cool drink, we can experience a deep feeling of contentment. A feeling of 'all's right with the world'.

We know that it is possible for the mind to flow, for it not to be involved in the pettiness of life, but to drift along with natural ease. We know these mental states are attainable and for the most part desirable, but they seem to come and go of their own accord. No matter how much we may want to experience a particular mental state, there is nothing that we can do that will, with any certainty, bring it about. We pursue the pleasant mental states we call happiness, at the expense of the unpleasant ones we call unhappiness. This is the action of a victim. We are tied to the notion of happiness in the same way a calf is tied to its mother.

We put our faith in an idea of happiness without understanding where real happiness lies.

A man was crawling on his hands and knees under a street light late one night.
A friend passed by and asked him what he was doing.
"I have dropped my key," said the man, "and I'm looking for it."
"Let me help you," said his friend.
The man and his friend searched for the key for almost an hour but could not find it. Eventually the friend said, "It doesn't seem to be here. Are you sure that this is where you dropped it?"
"Oh no," said the man, "I dropped it in the garden."
"Then why are we looking for it under this street light?" asked the friend.
"There is more light here," answered the man.

We seek happiness, but we look in the wrong place.

We are the cork and our mind is the wave. When the conditions are right, we ride on the crest of the wave. Everything is going well and life is good. When this changes as it must, we find ourselves in a trough, where nothing is right and the whole world is against us.

If we want to alter our status from servant to master of our mind, and then by extension, to our whole life, we have to undergo some training. We have to begin to de-condition the mind from its attachment to pleasant mental states and its aversion to unpleasant mental states. To find a point of balance. This is achieved through the profound practice of meditation called Vipassana.

Vipassana meditation works by allowing us to see the mind in its natural state without any desire to change it to something different. With training, we can surrender into the practice and begin to see the mind for what it really is. A constant stream of thoughts, moods, feelings and emotions. Nothing more.

If we consider the natural state of the mind to be like a pool of crystal clear water and our mental states are like coloured dyes dripped into it, it is easy to see the effect that even the smallest drop of dye would have.

And this is what is happening every second of the day.

The clarity of our mind is being obscured by the endless dripping of dyes into the water. With the practice of Vipassana meditation, we can gain the first level of understanding into this process.

As understanding develops through the simple practice of non-attached observation, we can begin to realise intuitively that we are not the mental states. We can begin to appreciate that anger and what we consider ourselves to be are in fact, two different things. To experience the mind state of anger does not mean that we must necessarily be angry. The mental state we experience and the effect of it are always two

separate events. This is true for everything.
Mental states arise and pass away. They all do. That is their nature.

As this truth becomes clearer to us, we will naturally stop choosing one thing over another. We will let go of this endless struggle. If they are all arising and passing away, why waste our time and energy trying to ensure that some will last forever, and others are pushed away as soon as they become evident.
When we don't mind what the mind presents, we can be happy.
Our habit of constantly choosing favourable mind states over unfavourable ones is the very reason for our feelings of unhappiness, discontent and disappointment. When we can experience directly for ourselves the true nature of the mind, it no longer has power over us. We have stopped being the victim. The mind can now present any mental state and we are able to recognise it for what it really is. A coloured dye dripped into a pool of clear water. Not 'me', not 'mine', not what 'I am'.

If we wake up in the morning and experience the mental state of depression or lethargy, as we might do on any Monday morning when we have to go back to work, we can just acknowledge this as depression or lethargy, and continue with our life. No need to react or become overwhelmed by it. We can treat it with kindness and respect, but no real interest. "Good morning, depression, please excuse me, but I can't stay to talk, I have to go to work."

This is how to be the master of the mind. Not to attempt to bully it into being the way you think it should be, but allowing it to be the way it is. When there is no preference about its contents, there is never a problem. This is the way to realise true and lasting happiness.

> The Great Way is not difficult.
> Just avoid picking and choosing.
>
> Zen Master Joshu

Our suffering only arises when we oppose the truth. To know the truth, we have to know this mind.

The purpose of Vipassana meditation then is not to create particular mental states. It is not to develop new depths of relaxation. It is not therapy.

The purpose of Vipassana meditation is to see, know and understand the mind moment after moment. Experiencing our thoughts, moods, feelings and emotions as simple disruptions to its natural calmness. Like the wind in the trees, or the waves in the ocean.

By knowing the mind, we are free from its influence and being free from it we will experience the real happiness of liberation.

14 - Being hard on yourself

*'Enlightenment only comes
when the desire for it has fallen away.'*

At one time there was an old monk living alone at the top of a great hill. This monk had trained hard in the spiritual disciplines all his life and was well accomplished. However, his final delusion was that he mistakenly thought himself to be completely enlightened. He wasn't, but he thought he was. At the same time there was a young boy living with the other monks at the bottom of the hill. Although this boy was only seven years old, he really was enlightened and because of this, knew the mind of the old monk and his last great delusion.
Acting only from compassion, he decided to help.
Starting out very early in the morning the young boy began to climb the hill. Higher and higher he went until finally, in the early evening, he arrived at the old monk's camp. Upon seeing the old monk sitting by the fire, the young boy called out a greeting.
"Good evening sir, how are you?" he said.
"Fine, fine," replied the old monk, "Come and join me."
The boy did as he was asked and the two of them began to talk and to pass the time together sitting in the glow of the open fire. Finally, the boy asked a question.
"Tell me sir," asked the boy, "Have you finished your journey?"
"Yes, yes," answered the old monk, "In fact, I arrived at full enlightenment some time ago."
"I see," said the boy, "And did you acquire the magical powers when you became enlightened?"
"Yes I did," said the old monk.

"Would you demonstrate them for me?" asked the boy, "For example, would you create a special image for me to see?"
"Nothing easier," said the monk, "What would you like?"
"How about a beautiful mountain pool with sparkling clear water, surrounded by trees and flowers," said the boy.
"No trouble" answered the old monk, and with a wave of his hand, there appeared in the distance the image exactly as described.
"Wonderful," said the boy, "Can you add some lotus plants and some small fishes and frogs?"
"Easy," said the old monk, and with another wave of his hand, the required image appeared.
"Just one more thing is needed to make it perfect," said the boy.
"Name it," said the monk.
"A young woman from the village, kneeling by the water combing her hair," the boy said.
"No problem," said the monk, and for a third time, he made a pass with his hand and the image appeared. This time however, something dramatic happened.
The moment the old monk saw the image of the beautiful young woman combing her hair by the water's edge, he was consumed by sexual desire. In the same instant the image disappeared and he realised that he was not enlightened.
He turned to the boy and thanked him for his teaching, understanding now exactly what had happened. The boy, acting again from compassion, was able to work with the old monk and in due course was able to show him how to realise true enlightenment for himself.

It is not uncommon for people new to Vipassana and Dhamma practice to feel that at the end of a peaceful and well focused meditation sitting, they have resolved some difficulty within themselves. This is really just due to the feelings that manifest after such a calm, peaceful sitting and have no basis in fact. We feel calm and relaxed and wonder how we could ever be angry again. The space in our mind, brought to light by the inner peace, encourages such thoughts. We may even think that this feeling will last forever. In some instances I am sure that this deep calmness of mind had been mistaken for the enlightenment experience itself. Because of the peaceful qualities of mind we now encounter, we believe that all our un-peaceful qualities have been eradicated, uprooted and released forever. In such a state we might even exclaim, 'I will never be angry again!'

I have often heard people say things like, 'Oh, I had a problem with worry, but it's resolved now', only to find a few days later that it has reappeared.

It is the same for all our negative states of mind. The positive ones we don't worry about. When they arise, we are always happy to see them. Misleading ourselves because of subtle feelings arising out of meditation is not uncommon and is usually just a sign of inexperience. It is here that we need the guidance of a loving and caring teacher.

At one time there was a great ocean liner in dry dock. The engines had stopped at sea and the ship had to be towed into harbour. The owner of this great vessel immediately called the best technicians in the land to fix it. They arrived in force, armed with the very latest technology, but nothing could be done. They tried and tried but the engines would not start.

Eventually, one of the technicians went to the owner and explained the situation.

"We have done everything we can," he said, "And nothing has worked. Now we don't know what else to do. The only thing we can suggest is that you call a local man in the town.

He is very old and has been around ships all his life. Perhaps he knows something that we don't."

The man was called, and arriving with just an old canvas bag under his arm, went immediately to the engine room. He walked around for a few minutes before stopping at a large pipe. Opening his bag he took out an old hammer. Standing silently for a moment with the hammer in his hand, he suddenly let out a yell and hit the pipe as hard as he could. The engines immediately roared into life. The old man put the hammer back in his bag and without saying a word, left the ship.

The owner was delighted until the next day when a bill arrived on his desk for £1000. Suddenly he was furious.

He called the old man into his office and asked for an explanation.

"How can you charge me £1000 for simply hitting a pipe with a hammer?" he asked.

"Oh, I'm sorry," said the old man, "That was my mistake."

And taking the bill wrote the following:

For hitting pipe with a hammer: £10

For knowing where to hit pipe with hammer: £990

Sometimes our meditation sit will be very calm and peaceful and we may think, like the old monk in the story, that our journey is completed. Or at least well underway.

It is not possible for us to know the depth of our mental feelings or emotions or what causes will make them arise. It is at times like these that we must remain open, loving and wise. It may be that in the moment, we seem to have resolved the particular tendency towards anger or greed, but just when we least expect it, it will rear its ugly head again and trap us. Powerfully and without warning!

There is a saying, old habits die hard, and this is the truth. The habits that we have cultivated in our life stay with us for a long time. We can release ourselves from their grasp, but this process may also take a long time. In the meantime, it is better not to make assumptions about our progress and be cautious.

For a time, I trained as a Buddhist monk in the Theravada tradition of Buddhism. It was my intention to be the best monk that I could be, out of respect for the Buddha, my own teacher, my wife and my friends, and so I undertook the 'samana' training.

Samana means, 'one whose senses are under control', and so I spent many hours each day in silence and in meditation, and always conducted myself with mindfulness and dignity. The result of this training was the very deep feeling of peace and calm. All desires and aversions seemed to have fallen away.

One day I was invited to attend a house blessing celebration with my teacher and another monk. This was a very special occasion for the Burmese lay people who were doctors and had just moved into a new house. They had invited many friends and relatives and everyone was dressed in their finest clothes. The ladies, in traditional Burmese costume, looked especially elegant.

Arriving late, the first thing to do was to eat. In the Theravada tradition of Buddhism, it is a monk's rule that no food should be taken after midday, and so in accordance with this, we were directed straight to the dining room.

The families must have been awake for many hours preparing the delicious food for our benefit. Huge amounts of salad, rice, noodles and vegetables were waiting for us on the fully laden dining-room table, and more elegantly dressed Burmese women waiting to serve us.

However, as we walked in, me deeply engrossed in my practice of mindfulness, something caught my eye.
There on a plate in the middle of the table was a chocolate eclair. It was the biggest eclair I have ever seen, filled with fresh cream and covered by a thick layer of chocolate. It was a type of food that I had not eaten for some time and so the moment my eye caught sight of this beautiful object, my mind screamed, 'I want that!'
We sat down and ate, having the most delicious food almost forced upon us, but I kept one eye on the eclair. I wanted it, and in some way felt sure that by looking at it I could make sure no one else took it.
The generosity of the Burmese people is well-known and finally, I could eat no more. The Burmese lay people had managed to fill at least one Buddhist monk to capacity and I was not able to take another mouthful.
The eclair was left on a plate, until, I suppose, someone else took it. With so much food inside me, I was definitely past caring about its destiny.

The point of this small story is to indicate that greed, the desire to get something to make us happy, is deeply rooted in all of us and just because it doesn't appear for some time, does not mean that it is finished. It only means that the conditions for its arising have not been present. We can only deal with unwholesome mind states when they actually become conscious.
Until then, we don't know if we have them or not. So we need to be on our guard, and be prepared for their arising. It is not safe to assume that our feelings of jealousy or fear, anger or greed have been completely dissipated Just because we haven't seen them for some time. They may still be there, lurking quietly in the background, just waiting for the right

moment to show themselves.

However, in their arising there is no need to feel a sense of failure in practice. This is our opportunity to see them for what they really are, not 'me', not 'mine', not what 'I am'.
Impersonal movements of mind arising due to conditions. Then we can respond.
When there is space in the mind from not attaching to our habit of grasping at things, we can see the situation as it is and so respond appropriately.
To take the eclair or to leave it, or to simply let go of the desire.
But first we must see.

When we are centred through our understanding of truth, we are in control. Not of the external situation, but of our relationship to it. It is only in the moment that we can let go.

Learn not to attach to the different aspects of mind as being 'me', or 'mine', and live peacefully with them. They are not the enemy. They are friends who come to show us the way. They show us exactly where our suffering lies. And our suffering is always centred in the belief that these things are what we are.
But these things are not what we are, they are only what we experience.

This takes practice. A lot of practice, but liberation from the clutch is within our own hands. No one can do it for us.

The disappointment felt when realising that something once thought finished is in fact still present in our lives, can be immense, so it is better not to make assumptions. Live as

though these things are still realities for us, and respond accordingly. In this way we let go of our suffering and experience the joy of liberation.
Slowly, slowly, with love and patience.

Enlightenment only comes when the desire for it has fallen away. So relax, be easy with yourself. There is nothing for you to get, only that which can be realised.

15 - Not this

*'The world that we experience is the one
that we create for ourselves moment after moment.'*

A disciple went to his master one day and asked, "Master, what am I?"
The master replied, "Not this."
On hearing these words, the disciple was enlightened.

Often when we come to spiritual practice, we bring with us many of the big unanswered questions of life. Questions like the one in the story, 'What am I?' It is a very good question, very deep and very profound. We assume that we must be something. After all, we are alive, we think, we feel, we react. We sense that there must be an answer and hopefully through patient investigation, we can find this answer and know the truth.

Vipassana is the beginning of the answer.

Although in modern times Vipassana is generally understood to be a meditation practice, this is not true. The word itself means 'to see things as they really are', and anything that brings us to the point of clearly seeing and experiencing our own reality, can be called Vipassana.
The practice of Vipassana is not only about sitting cross-legged on the floor, watching the breath in the nostrils and the sensations in the body. It is about life itself.
Vipassana is a unique approach to life and living. Through the development of love and awareness we are able to live in the world peacefully and harmoniously, sharing happiness

and joy with all beings.

Fundamentally, Vipassana asks one question: 'When the only thing I want in life is to be happy all the time, why can't I be?' In other words, 'What is the cause of my unhappiness?'

Through the meditation practice, we can begin to see and understand the cause of unhappiness. Once known and comprehended, we are able to do something about it, namely let it go. Release it from our life and be free from it!

Love and awareness are the most important requirements of spiritual development, for without them we can never proceed beyond the limitations we place upon ourselves. With wisdom, we know how to live in the world. With love, we do not insist that others follow our way. To reach this beautiful point of realisation we have to understand the truth, and this understanding comes only from a personal and consistent investigation of the mind. To see things as they really are.

This is not an intellectual or academic pursuit. It is not a theory or speculation. It is a direct investigation into this being that we call 'self', and only we can do it. No matter how much we may wish it, no-one can do this practice for us. And of course, it probably will mean long hours of sitting still, not speaking or being distracted and just observing the forces that propel us through our life. These forces originate in the mind, and our habit is to empower each one that arises and so make it a unique reality for us.

The world that we experience is the one that we create for ourselves moment after moment.

This must be truly understood.

To be free from our pain, suffering, discontent and unhappiness in life we must end our attachment to the mind and body as being who and what we are. There is no other way.

True Vipassana, once begun, is relentless. It is not a panacea or therapy. Vipassana has only one function, and that is to awaken us to the truth.

Whoever or whatever you think you are, you are not. It is only mind arising and passing away.

We need the mind, of course. We don't have to abandon it or change it or give it up, in fact, we don't have to do anything with it.

Mind is just mind. We don't have to manipulate it to get something better. The truth is that there nothing to get, not even enlightenment.

And actually enlightenment isn't the point. The desire to attain some special state is the very thing that will prevent it from happening. It's like trying to walk to the horizon. It just can't be done. So in Vipassana practice, we just live according to our understanding that whatever we attach to will hurt us. This also includes any attachment to an idea of enlightenment. As our attachments fall away, our life becomes more flowing and fulfilling and we forget about enlightenment. Then it can happen.

Before it happens, it is beyond our limited human comprehension. After it happens - it's just enlightenment.

When a Japanese Zen master was asked, "What is it like to be enlightened?"
He replied, "In summer we sweat, in winter we freeze."

Just like everyone else. The difference is that there is no attachment to either state. There is only one peaceful response to the ever-changing conditions. This is the point of practice. We have to understand that the Buddha did not get enlightenment, he realised it, and this only happened when he gave up the search for it. It was something he already had, not something he had to create.

This is me, but it's not what I am.

Do you understand?

'This is me', is the mental state present in this moment, but it will not and cannot last. Its true nature is to be impermanent. 'But it's not what I am', is our relationship to it.
This is me but it's not what I am.

However, our attachment or identification to mind and body is extremely strong and although the teachings of Vipassana are very simple, they are never easy. Breaking habits never is. But we start slowly, and continue with determination. If we want to change our life we can, but only if we truly want it. This is the most important point to understand, is this what we really want?

Everything is already in place, just waiting for us to collect. There is nothing to get and nothing to be done. Only breaking our attachment. And this is liberation.
Because of the liberating process of dropping attachment there is the supreme freedom to live in the world. A freedom that is not conditioned by the past, and not in anticipation of the future. A freedom that allows life itself to unfold spontaneously, moment after moment, bringing with it the ability to enjoy all the wonderful things that can be enjoyed, with the strength to endure all the unpleasant things that still have to be endured. Patiently and without complaint. Before

we experience the liberating quality of Vipassana we cannot even begin to comprehend a life free from attachment. Once we do experience it however, it seems normal. It becomes our usual way to live.

Of course, our habit of holding onto things that actually causes pain is very strong. Look at our relationships. We very often cling to them long after they have any positive value.

Like a story of the young woman, who was told by her boyfriend to leave him.

"I think we should separate," he said, "Because our relationship is not making you happy."

"But I don't want to be happy," she replied, "I want to stay with you."

In the end our happiness or lack of it, comes entirely from ourselves. No one else is responsible for how we feel or what we do. All our feelings and actions come only from ourselves. When we understand this, we are able to live a life that is free from blaming and judging others and where we no longer feel ourselves to be the victim in any situation. This is the beauty of Vipassana.

To be strong, and yet gentle, open and non judgemental, able to live in this world fully and freely with love and awareness and so not be lost in the delusions of mind.

Vipassana never tells you what you are, it only ever shows you what you are not.

What are you? Not this!

Be happy.

16 - Everything is best

'Watching the breath for its own sake seems pointless.'

At one time a disciple was walking through a market. As he was passing the butchers stall he overheard a conversation between the butcher and his customer.
"Give me the best piece of meat you have," said the customer.
"Everything on my stall is the best," replied the butcher, "You cannot find one piece of meat here that is not the best."
Upon hearing these words, the mind of the disciple was opened and pure understanding arose.

It is a natural tendency for each one of us to always want the best. It is part and parcel of our social conditioning. To succeed our parents, to have more and better of everything. My own father told me on many occasions that it was his wish for me to have all the things that he could not have when he was young. As parents, I think we all carry this way of thinking.
We usually equate having the best with happiness and so it is our natural desire for us to want the best for ourselves and then by extension, for our families and friends. This way of thinking can develop and grow, so that it also includes our own particular social or ethnic group as well as many other sections of global society.
With this attitude, we always want the best for our group or association and always experiencing unhappiness and the feelings of dissatisfaction when we have to 'make do', have to accept something that is not the best.

In spiritual practice also, the desire to always have the best can become a prominent way of thinking. Wanting the best teacher, the best and most profound school tradition or spiritual training with the best kind of enlightening experiences. And why not? If society encourages all of us to actively seek the very best for ourselves, why should we not incorporate that attitude into our spiritual training? It doesn't seem to be unreasonable.

Even when we come together to meditate and sit as a group, we can see others (and if we look really closely, ourselves) actively seeking the best. We want the best cushion to sit on, and we want it in the best place. Near to the window if it's warm, and near to the radiator if it is too cold. Not too close to the front in case we are called upon to say something and not too near the back in case we can't hear what's being said. Also, we don't want to sit close to anyone who breathes heavily or who falls asleep and snores, as sometimes happens. In short, we are all looking for perfect conditions to train under. We are all looking for the best.

Many years ago, when I would have to practice meditation in my bedroom in the evening, I had a real experience of how far the mind will go in its attempt to get the best. To create the perfect conditions for practice.

On this occasion, a warm summer's evening, I had just begun to sit when things began to go wrong. First the sun moved its position in the sky to shine brightly in my face. This very quickly became annoying, but my mind came up with the answer. What I really needed was a small remote control unit directly in front of me, so that by simply extending a finger I could press a button and the curtains would close. Perfect.

As the sun continues to shine through the window, the temperature increased and I began to feel the heat. This called for another button on my imaginary remote control unit. This time I could turn on a fan in the ceiling so that the gentle movement of air would cool me. Again, perfect.

Later, the neighbour's dog was allowed out to spend the next ten minutes playing and barking in the garden below. What I needed now was another button to operate some kind of sound proofing device on the windows. This would solve that problem.

And so it went on. Each interruption or difficulty encountered could be met and overcome by the addition of another button on my imaginary remote control unit. The final thing was the darkness. As the sun began to set and the room became darker, I realised that I needed another button to turn on the light. That will be the last addition, just one more thing and everything would be perfect.

In my mind, the tendency to seek perfect conditions knew no bounds. I had managed to spent a full hour completely missing what was actually happening and spent the time mentally creating a set of imaginary conditions. Happily, I realised very quickly that the list we create in our mind for things to be right for our spiritual practice and indeed life itself, can be endless. And as soon as we think it is complete, we add something else to it. Another button on our personal remote control unit.

When it comes to our mental states we also seek perfection. We want everything to be just right.

To sit and watch our breath is fine as long as it goes somewhere, as long as it takes us to where we want to go. Watching the breath for its own sake seems pointless. We want our mind to become calm and peaceful, so that we leave our meditation in a state of deep relaxation. We want to feel that we have got the best out of it.

If we come to our meditation practice with the idea that we

can achieve calm and peaceful mental states by following the rhythm of the breath in the nostrils, we will be disappointed if it doesn't happen. To sit in a state of expectancy, not really focusing our attention on the work in hand, but waiting for the special, pleasant and possibly deeply spiritual experiences to happen.

Daily life is the same. There is always the feeling of discontent and disappointment if the condition of the mind is anything but radiant through the feelings of happiness. Here too, we always want to experience only the best. None of us ever want to suffer the feelings of depression, sorrow or irritation. We only ever pursue their opposites such as joy, happiness and all the other positive states of mind. When we find that we can't control the mental states that we are experiencing, we become despondent and downhearted and resign ourselves to suffering until it passes. It is the same for all of us. It is not possible to control our mind, so that we can choose the mental state we wish to experience. If it were possible, we would all, without exception, upon waking in the morning choose to be happy all day.

So the point here is that we all have to work with whatever is presented to us in the field of spiritual development. Whether our cushion is too high or too low was not the point. Whether we sit in our favourite place or not, is not the point. Whether our mind is thinking of a hundred different ways to get out of the meditation hall without losing face, is not the point. The point is to observe and experience the natural movement of mind as it struggles to organise and control everything. As it seeks out what it thinks is the best for itself.

The goal of practice is to relax and be at peace with the mind as it is. When we stop trying to control everything that arises we can actually experience for ourselves the truth that 'everything is teaching us something, if only we had the eyes to see it'.

Whatever is happening right now is the best for us and if we no longer resist surrendering to it, we will be able to accept and be peaceful with it.

So our attitude in practice - and practice is not separate from daily life - is to be open to the changing conditions of mind. To observe them, to be fully aware of them, but not to make a fuss. Pleasant mental states come and go, so do unpleasant ones, and none of them stay forever.

Once we can allow everything to develop naturally, there is no more fighting, no more resisting and no more looking for the best. Just an acceptance of how things really are and how we can learn from them.

17 - Letting go

'Give up trying to shape the universe to suit yourself and be happy.'

At one time there were two friends in Japan. Often they would spend time together, enjoying the company and friendship of each other. However, one of the two was blind, and one evening when visiting his friend he stayed late and darkness had fallen.

In those days, the only way to light your way home was to carry a paper and bamboo lantern with a lighted candle inside. The sighted friend offered one to his blind companion.

"Of what use is that to me?" said the blind man, "dark or light is all the same, a lantern is the last thing I need."

"I know that you do not need a lantern for yourself," his friend replied, "but please take this so that others may see you and not run into you."

So the blind friend took the lantern and set off into the night. He had not gone very far when someone ran squarely into him, knocking him to the ground.

"Look out!" he shouted angrily, "can't you see my lantern?"

"I'm sorry brother," came back the strangers voice, "but your candle has gone out."

The way that we usually live in the world is to place ourselves directly at the centre, and then demand that everyone and everything pleases and satisfies us.

We always believe that our views and opinions are the best and because of that, all others are inferior. We all know that, given the opportunity, we could soon 'put the world to rights' and if only everyone would follow our design for life, we could all be happy. We believe that our way is right and all other ways are wrong. This is not only experienced in the West. It is a universal condition of human beings. Men and women alike.

From birth, we are told who we are, what we are and how to behave. We are instructed in what is acceptable and what is not. We are conditioned. As we grow from childhood we carry this early conditioning with us, always reinforcing and developing it through contact with others of a like mind and culture, our own particular family, social group and of course, the media. As we grow older, these views and opinions become firmly established and we can feel a sense of security in the knowledge that not only is there a set order to our particular universe, but we are truly a part of it.

This is why so many old people feel threatened by the young. They are the unknown quantity that can upset the status quo. We all carry the feeling that our way, and only our way is right. That is the bottom line.

The first time I was in India, my sensibilities were disturbed by some of the customs I encountered there. What is considered normal social behaviour by Indians is not always accepted as polite manners by Westerners. However, being in that environment for some months, one becomes not only used to seeing things that were once difficult to accept, but gradually living peacefully with them. Eventually, as demonstrated by some Westerners who had been India for a very long time, these habits become the norm for them too.

In those days, as a highly conditioned British citizen, I prided myself on my ability to queue. This is a universal mark of British people, the ability to stand in line waiting for an official to deal with us. This habit however, has not been taken up by the Indian people, and so attempting to buy a train ticket can be a very long process as only Europeans will queue. The Indians go straight to the front of the line to be served.

At first all the Westerners new to India become very irate, not being used to this kind of treatment. Soon however, experience dictates and everyone pushes forward, as is the social convention. It takes some doing, but eventually it becomes the normal and accepted way to queue.

Also in India, there are no litter bins. The people use what they want and throw the rubbish onto the streets. Actually, this isn't as bad as it sounds, as the freely wandering cows, dogs and rats eat what can be eaten and the rest is swept into little heaps and burned. Not a bad system. However, you can always find Westerners walking around with a handful of rubbish, afraid to drop it. Eventually we learn. Eventually we go against our conditioning.

As my time in India was drawing to a close, I found myself quite upset at the prospect of returning home. I had not only grown used to life in India, but actually enjoyed it very much. However, the startling thing upon arriving in England was the experience of culture shock. It was literally stepping into another world.

The point about this observation regarding the difference between two cultures is that when one becomes used to what was once a completely opposing set of moral or social standards, they become not only acceptable, but the norm. The right way not only for ourselves, but by extension, for everyone else too.

My reaction to Western female fashion, having spent six months in India was something along the lines of, 'Oh they shouldn't be dressed like that. They should wear something more modest. What will their mothers think?'

Then their mothers would come out of the shop behind them wearing something almost identical. Very confusing.
Unless we can let go of trying to organise everyone and everything to suit our own particular ideas of how we think they should be, we will always be struggling.

In Dharamsala in northern India, where I stayed for some time, all the water pipes that feed the town run up and down the main street on the surface. Not neatly hidden as they would be in the West, but running in groups of ten or fifteen narrow pipes, some on the left side of the street, some on the right. Very easy to trip over if you were not careful. Also the streets were always wet and muddy because most of the pipes leaked.
This not only produced frustration on the faces of the Western men staying in Dharamsala, but you could hear it often in conversations.
'What these people need to do is to get themselves organised, spend some money and have these pipes buried underground. It is not right to leave things like this'.
These people were really suffering. The Tibetans on the other hand, who are the main inhabitants of Dharamsala, didn't seem to mind at all. The Westerners were suffering but the Tibetans were happy. There is a lesson here.
Give up trying to shape the universe to suit yourself and be happy. Let go of this attachment that only your ideas and opinions have value. Relax, then everything takes its course.

The Tao te Ching, the ancient Chinese manual of wisdom asks, 'Do you think you can take over the universe and improve it?' and then answers for itself, 'I do not believe it can be done'.
The universe goes its own way, unhindered by the likes and

dislikes of ourselves.

The weather is as it is, whether we have a picnic planned or not. The sports results come in as they are no matter which teams we support. Our life, and the life of all those we hold near and dear, is subject to the same uncertainties as everyone elses.

The goal of human life is happiness.
We all want it and we all do whatever we can to get it.
In our mind we carry a blueprint for happiness and we know exactly how everything should be for ourselves and for the rest of the world in order for that experience to arise. It is not wrong to want happiness but it is misguided to think that there will ever be a time when we can organise everyone and everything that exists in such a way as to be perfect for us. Remember, everyone else is trying to do the same thing.

We have to let go of trying to shape everyone and everything to suit our own idea and let nature take its course. We have to allow things to unfold naturally, and not interfere.

It is said that if God controls the universe,
He does it by allowing everything to happen.

Usually when things go wrong, we blame others. This is a normal reaction and it is sure that everyone has said on one occasion or another, 'It's your fault I'm angry', or 'I feel like this because of what you said (or did)', always blaming the other for the mental state we are experiencing. This is a huge delusion!

Although external influences are always triggers and conditions for our mental states, we are always responsible for our reactions. To say that something outside ourselves has produced a feeling of anger or irritation is not only incorrect. It is actually impossible.

Anger, and all mental states, begin and end within us. Not outside, not by people, events or situations, but within us. By our own reactions. By our habits of wanting things our own way, whether on a gross level or a subtle one.

We are always responsible for ourselves.

It is a fact that we choose one type of mental state over another. We always choose a pleasant one over an unpleasant one. This is our human nature and it is reflected in every aspect of life. Pleasant mental states we call happiness, unpleasant mental states we call unhappiness. It is the choosing between them that causes the suffering.

Zen Master Joshu said:
The great way is simple,
it only means giving up picking and choosing.

If we really want to be at peace with ourselves and then by extension, the whole universe, we have to let go of trying to control everything. For this to happen we must begin with our own mind. This means that we have to allow the mind to be exactly as it is without making choices and distinctions as to how we think it should be.

The practice we use to develop this profound understanding of reality is known as Insight Meditation (Vipassana) and is the way of being at peace with things exactly as they are, without insisting that they be different, just to suit ourselves. The result of the cultivation of this form of meditation is a more open and relaxed attitude to life, having established acceptance of the natural tendencies of mind.

In short, it is peace.

A way to exist in the world without forcing our ideas and views upon others and a way to live comfortably with the many things that cause us pain or discomfort. It means not to indulge in flights of fancy about the universe and everything in it, and to accept and take the responsibility for ourselves and how we live.

It means to understand the truth that we are the architects and creators of our own life and no one is responsible for us, but ourselves.

PART TWO

A meeting with the Buddha
A Dhamma journey

Not This

Introduction

Taken from a Dhamma talk given at the Isle of Man Buddhist group, May 1992.

This is not a work of fact, nor is it a work of fiction.
This is simply a series of images and ideas presented in modern terms, concerning a meeting between Gotama, the historical Buddha, and yourself.
You are the leading character in this story and your goal is to receive a teaching from the lips of an enlightened being. From your first encounter with one of his close followers through the different people you meet, his teaching is slowly revealed to you until finally you can sit at his feet yourself and hear his own words.
The teaching presented here, although couched in modern language is accurate and comes from the author's long years of study and practice in the tradition of Theravada Buddhism, both as a monk and a layman. The final teachings are taken from the first chapter of the Dhammapada, a section of the Suttanta Pitika and part of the Theravada Buddhist scriptures.

This small discourse may be read as a guided meditation, sharing each moment to reveal the depth of wisdom behind the Buddha's teachings with each sentence taking you nearer to the Buddha himself.
The words are meant to be enjoyed and appreciated, but more importantly applied to everyday life. For this is the essence of the teaching of the Buddha.

The beginning

Let our story begin.
Imagine, it is night...

This night like so many other nights, you have lain in your simple bed gazing at the stars through the window, unable to sleep.
It is curious. Your family and friends have always been able to accept the way that life has been presented and to be at ease with the traditions that have been handed down through generations. But for you it's different. You have never been able to accept something simply because everyone else does. Your father calls you awkward and contrary, but there is nothing intentional on your part. Just the misgivings you feel from accepting things without fully understanding them.
You want to know about life. You need to know, and it is this very need that keeps you awake at night.

Why is life the way it is?
Why does it seem to be a happy and fortunate affair for some, and yet for others contain nothing but pain and misery? What is the reality behind the apparent unfairness of life. Why are things like this, and what is the point of it all anyway, if the only thing that we can be sure of is death?
You feel that there is an answer to these questions and that answer could be found if only someone would point out the right direction and the right path.
To your village come many wandering teachers, each claiming themselves to be enlightened and to have the only true path, but their words are so different.

When the famous naked ascetic, Purana Kassapa arrived at the outskirts of the village you had immediately rushed to offer alms and to hear him speak. Yet, when he did speak his words left you cold.
He told you and the few others that had assembled, that there was neither punishment for wrong deeds done, nor reward for any kind actions, and that in life no restraints need be placed upon any desire to hurt or harm others. Any action can be taken at any time without fear of spiritual retribution.
You had left shaking your head. How can this be so? Even the child feels the pricks of conscience when it has done something wrong.

Later, when another famous teacher arrived at the village with his followers you again had rushed to hear him speak, but once more met only disappointment.
Makkhali Gosala had spoken only of predestination. That the life of all beings is fixed and nothing can alter this. No man can become enlightened, unless it is written in the pages of destiny. This is our lot.
Again, you walked away shaking your head. How can this be so? There has to be a way to liberation for all men.

And so it was with other well respected teachers arriving at your village. Each one with their disciples and supporters, claiming to have discovered the answers to the deepest questions of life, only to expound a personal theory or philosophy that did not inspire you to examine that particular teaching more closely. Theories of annihilation, the causelessness of effects and the randomness of the universe. All expounded with conviction, and vigour, yet none of them touching your heart.

However, today in the early morning as you were returning from bathing, a new experience concerning the teaching of others confronted you.

Standing quietly at the open door of a house was an unusual wanderer. Without asking for alms he waited a moment and then moved on. At the next house he was offered some cooked rice which he accepted into his bowl and yet said nothing. Nor did he lift his eyes from the ground, but silently replaced the lid of his bowl and moved on.
His manner was humble and kindly, and his appearance simple and clean. He wore only a patched orange robe and sported a shaven head, identifying him as a disciple of the teacher Gotama, said by some to be a living Buddha.

For you, inspired by the manner and bearing of this quiet and peaceful man, this was an opportunity not to be missed.

Waiting for him to finish his alms round, you had discreetly followed him back to the river where silently and with great good manners he ate his small meal.
When his meal was finished and his bowl rinsed in the river, he sat beneath a tree to rest and allow his food to digest. This was your chance and so, with much deference and hesitation, you approached. Kneeling and placing your palms together in an attitude of respect you began to speak.

"Bhante," you said, "I have been searching for answers to many spiritual questions for a long time now and I would consider it a privilege if you would speak to me."
The wanderer said nothing but merely smiled and motioned for you to sit down.
How different this was from the other teachers you have

sought out, who wasted not a moment to proclaim their own importance and superiority. But this man said nothing, waiting patiently for you to begin.

"Bhante, many, many teachers come to our small village to expound their own teachings and philosophies. Each one so different and yet each one claiming that theirs is the only truth and always criticising the words of others. I listen to them, always hoping to find a teaching that I can adhere to, but always come away confused by the contradictions inherent in their philosophies. May I ask Bhante, who is your teacher, and what is the teaching he proclaims?"

The wanderer sat in silence. There was no rush here to expound a favourite theory or speculation. Just patience and peace.

"My teacher is Gotama the Buddha, at this moment residing two days journey from here. I am on my way to join him. His teaching is one of liberation for all men and women, regardless of race or caste and success is assured for those who would simply follow his words and make their own effort.

The path laid down by Gotama is one that transcends any form of extreme behaviour and insists upon the cultivation of a natural virtue and high moral standards. This is combined with the devoted practice of meditation, following a technique discovered by himself. The result of these two practices is peace and wisdom as the ignorance that binds us all to the wheel of suffering is eradicated little by little. This in brief is the teaching of Gotama, and you yourself are to be commended for your hesitation in accepting the words and ideas of others, simply because of their reputation or style, or even because it has been handed down by tradition to follow them. Gotama has told his followers to question and examine all things. This includes his own teachings, for he does not consider blind faith complimentary to the spiritual path. It is only when such teachings can be considered beautiful, blameless and worthy in one's own heart, should they be pursued."

With this, the wanderer fell silent again, waiting for the possibility of further questions.
For you, this was a revelation. No blind faith here, and liberation from the suffering and difficulties of life. This was a teaching you must pursue further.

You must hear the Buddha speak.

Having discovered the exact location of Gotama, you again pay your respects to the lone wanderer and make your way back to your home. Your mind is aflame at the prospect of hearing in person, the architect of a spiritual path that leads to the end of suffering for all beings.

These thoughts had consumed you throughout the day and even now would not let you sleep. However one thing was certain now, as the dawn light began to fill the night sky, today would be the beginning of your journey to sit at the feet of a so-called 'living Buddha'.

> People without awareness
> do not see the truth,
> and, as only a few birds
> escape the fowlers net,
> so too only a few
> see the potential of their life.

Dhammapada: verse 174

Not This

The journey (1)

Your journey begins with the farewells to your family.
They can't understand why you have to go away so suddenly. You try to explain that for you, this is not sudden at all, but simply the final brush stroke to a painting you have been hoping to finish for many years. And in any case, you're not going away for ever. Just a few days to hear a teacher talk about the meaning of our existence.

Your father is not convinced of the wisdom of your plan, and walks away mumbling about traditions and how they have served the people adequately for generations. Why then do the young have to go against what is well established, just to satisfy their own curiosity?
However, he begrudgingly wishes you good luck and a safe journey.
Your mother is quiet, realising the desire that is in you. She offers you a small bag containing some food and a few coins to help you on your way. Thanking her and saying goodbye to your brothers and sisters you leave the house eager to start your journey.

The excitement that is in you generates much energy and ignoring the heat of the day you walk quickly, soon reaching the next village. Stopping to eat a little food and drink some water you begin a conversation with some of the men.

"I am travelling to hear Gotama, the teacher," you reply when asked about your journey, "I have met and spoken to one of his followers and was impressed by what he told me. Now I feel I must hear him speak in person."

"Ah yes," they reply in unison nodding their heads, "That Gotama has a good reputation. It is said that he was a Prince of the Sakya clan, but renounced everything for the holy life. Imagine that, renouncing the life of a Prince to live in poverty. He must be very wise," they said, "or very stupid." They all laughed at that, slapped your back and wished you good fortune as you continued on your way.

The day wears on and by the evening you have reached the next village. Tired and weary, you hope for a little hospitality and somewhere to sleep. You are not disappointed, for the people are friendly and offer you everything that you need. The villagers here are also curious about you and where you are going. Once again you explain your intentions, and the people mumble their approval. This time however, you meet with a pleasant surprise, a lone voice come from the darkness and makes a simple yet dynamic statement.
"Gotama, I have seen and heard him."
Seen and heard him! This was fantastic. Someone who has seen and heard a man, who is called by some the living Buddha. You have to know more.
"Yes," the voice continues, "I was working for a merchant when we arrived at the place where Gotama was staying with some of his followers. The word in the town was that he would give a talk that evening to the people, so I went along. You know, I've always been interested in these so-called 'holy men'. A lot of them don't seem to be so holy to me, but this one was different.
He spoke very simply, so that even the most stupid of us could understand his message. And he didn't once stop to beat his chest or puff himself up to impress his audience. He just said what he said and then was silent.
Even when some of the rich Brahmins challenged him, there

was not a hint of anger or impatience. Just peacefulness. It seemed to flow out of him and down onto us.
I was very taken by him.
One Brahmin challenged him and asked about the merits gained through sacrificing animals, you know, how much is a goat worth, how much is a horse worth, that sort of thing? Gotama said that if we really wanted to make merit through sacrifice, we should sacrifice our own desires and greed, and our own dislikes and aversions. In this way we will cultivate true merit by living in the world in a kind and selfless way and by helping other beings less fortunate than ourselves.
The Brahmins didn't seem to like that very much, but when I spoke with the people afterwards, many said how much he had touched their heart. A lot of people that night became lay supporters of Gotama, and some even went to ask if they could become his close followers, have their heads shaved and wear the orange robe. He calls them 'bhikkhus', you know, beggars, but I don't think they are allowed to beg. I don't think they are allowed to ask for anything except water and medicine. They have to wait for everything to be offered freely. I have heard many holy men speak, but non have impressed me as much as this wanderer Gotama. Some say he is the living Buddha and I believe it to be true."

For a moment in the silence, intensified by the darkness of the evening, everything stops. No thoughts, no dreams, no plans. Just peace and contentment.

The living Buddha.

To sit at the feet of a living Buddha could be the reason for life itself.
If there had been a moment's doubt in your mind about the

purpose of your journey, tonight it had been dispelled. Now the fire to be with Gotama was burning in your heart more fiercely than ever.

Gradually, you become aware of the voices again. Inspired by the lone speaker, they all begin to recount second and third hand stories of holy men.
But for you only further discussion with the lone voice will do. You seek him out and question him late into the night. He says that he is happy to talk and tells you that one day when the time is right and his children are grown and can care for their mother, he will leave the family life and seek acceptance as a disciple of Gotama, such was the impact of this teacher upon him.

With the breaking of dawn comes the continuation of your journey. Waving goodbye to new friends you set out again down the long dusty road that leads the next village.

> It is wise to live a virtuous life
> and always have confidence in the Dhamma.
> But it is only through wisdom
> that happiness beyond personal limitations,
> will appear.

Dhammapada: verse 333

The journey (2)

Minute after minute, footstep after footstep your journey continues, each mile taking you nearer to the camp of the Buddha.

Somewhere along the road you meet another traveller.

An old man, walking slowly in the heat of the day, coming from the village you are going to. You stop to share some food and water and again to your delight, you find yourself with another person who has heard Gotama speak.

"Yes, I have heard him," he says, "A few days ago outside our village. He gave a very good talk. Very interesting. Very inspiring. Many of the younger men who were there were so inspired that they wanted to join his close followers immediately, but he told them that they must first receive permission from their parents. I don't think many other holy men would have said that you know, telling interested people to reflect and receive permission, but he didn't seem interested in simply swelling his numbers. His message was different.
He told us that not everyone has the opportunity to abandon the home life, and it's true, many of us have families and responsibilities that it would be difficult to simply walk away from, even for enlightenment, and he seemed to recognise that.
For those of us in that position, he offered five rules of training, which if applied to our daily life would without doubt, improve its quality, and not just our own life, but by extension, the lives of all those around us.

The first training rule is about killing and harming living beings.
He pointed out that all creatures want to live just as much as we do, and no living thing enjoys pain. If we remember how we like to be treated and apply that to all beings everyone will be much happier.
The second training rule was not to steal or even take things before they are offered. For most of us, possessions are few and have been hard to come by. We treasure our things in the same way that others treasure theirs. It is the same for all of us. When we realise how we would feel if somebody stole any of our belongings, we would never take something from somebody else, without their permission or consent.
The next training rule that he shared with us is about sex and adultery. You know, infidelity brings only pain and disgrace to everyone concerned, but especially the parents and guardians of young women. He reminded us of what we already know in our hearts, that it is better to treat wives, daughters and husbands with love and respect and stay faithful to them.

The fourth training rule was about speech. He reminded us of the damage that we can do by simply using our speech in the wrong way. Back-biting, telling lies carrying tales and idle gossip. These ways of talking can be very hurtful, and it is hard to see how anyone benefits from such action. He told us that we should try to use our speech only in a good and useful way. To bring harmony to each situation and to unite people, not cause further trouble.

The last training rule he talked about, was drugs. You know, drinking alcohol and smoking marijuana, that kind of thing. Most of us enjoy a drink at least after a hard day's work, but Gotama said that these things only serve to cloud our mind and actually obscure reality. If we haven't got a clear mind to see how things really are how can we improve the quality of our life? Also, in many cases, drink makes men argumentative, sometimes leading to fighting and then feeling too ill to work the next day. You don't have to be enlightened to know that, but still, we act as though it is not true.

He said that if we can learn to let go of our selfish impulses and desires and follow these five guidelines our lives will become more peaceful and harmonious and we will be able to accumulate great merit."

The old man then fell silent. He took a mouthful of water and looked back along the road he had come.

"If I were a younger man, I think I would have joined the others in trying to become one of his close followers, but still, he has given me a lot to think about in my last few years."

"Will you go to hear him speak again?" you ask.

"Oh yes, he replies, "Any time, any time at all."

With that old man takes his leave. You watch him as he slowly disappears into the haze on the horizon.

For you, still sitting at the side of the road, your mind is alive with the words you have heard. The prospect of hearing the original speaker in person excites and elates you more than ever.

Tomorrow. Perhaps tomorrow you will meet Buddha.

> Let go of unwholesome actions.
> Cultivate wholesome actions.
> Purify your own mind.
> These are the teaching of all
> Awakened beings.
>
> Dhammapada: verse 183

The meeting

As the early afternoon of the next day develops, you arrive at the small town where the Buddha is reputed to be. This place, by comparison to your own village, is large and bustling with people. So many different castes, colours. So many different sounds and dialects.
For you this is all part of the adventure.
You wander around the market spending the few coins given to you by your mother and begin to make inquiries about Gotama. People gather around you, happy to give information, requested or not, telling stories and asking questions about your journey. Finally however, you manage to find the location of Gotama's camp just outside the town. Tonight there will be a talk, they say. It will begin just after sunset.

Now you can hardly contain yourself.

You wander to the river to eat the small amount of food you have left and to wash off some of the dust and tiredness of your journey. For you now, the evening cannot come quickly enough.
Having eaten and bathed you rest, waiting impatiently for the light to leave the sky.

Finally the sun begins to lower itself on the horizon and it is dusk.
In the distance, you see small groups of people and hear their hushed voices. Everywhere there is a feeling of peace and stillness. The time you have been waiting for has arrived.
You stand, stretch yourself and follow the people in their

irregular procession. Some smile and nod at you, whilst others keep themselves to themselves, but all of them with great respect, head for the camp of the Buddha.

Entering a clearing in the sparse forest that borders the town, you find yourself transported, almost to another world.
At the far end, there is a cloth canopy standing over a slightly raised mound of earth. This has been covered with pieces of simple fabric and small oil lamps have been fixed to supports at each end. Without question this is the place where the Buddha will teach.

As the people begin to settle in groups at different parts of the clearing you make your way forward, not quite to the front but close, close enough to see this man and hear every word he will say. A feeling of deep peacefulness fills this place and spontaneously without any instruction, the people wait in silence.
Then from the distance comes the sound of someone clearing their throat, and the rustle of robes. This is the signal. It is beginning.

From the gloom beyond the platform, a silent procession of the Buddha disciples, the bhikkhus, come into the clearing and take their places around the platform, facing the place where the Buddha will sit and with their backs to you.
When they are settled, more bhikkhus appear from the shadows, again in silence, and they position themselves on the platform leaving a space around the central cushions already prepared for perhaps, three or four more people. Now your heart is racing. The excitement, the anticipation and the joy of being in this place, surge up from somewhere deep inside to overwhelm you.

You find yourself smiling without knowing why, and straining your eyes into the darkness behind the platform to see what lies beyond.

Finally, ending the moment that seemed to last forever, more figures emerge from the darkness. Four men, identical to each other and to the bhikkhus that preceded them, arrange themselves in the central position on the platform. Three sit and one stands slightly to the rear of the middle figure. The bhikkhu standing holds a large fan which he gently begins to move through the air, causing the faintest of breezes to fall onto the body of the central figure.
That of Gotama. The living Buddha.

Now, you sit quietly.
The excitement and anticipation fade and a peacefulness never before experienced envelops you. Your breathing becomes calmer and deeper as you wait for the words to begin.
The presence of Gotama is overwhelming. His stature is that of an ordinary man, and yet he seems to fill the whole grove. The flickering light from the lamps falls onto his face, illuminating his pleasant features, emphasising the feeling of closeness. Although this place is filled with people, some seekers like yourself, some interested passers-by and some simply curious, you know that each one has the feeling as you do, the Gotama is here just for them.
How could it be otherwise?

The people wait in silence. Nobody shuffles or clears their throat or coughs. Everyone simply waits.

After what seemed an age, Gotama the living Buddha, begins

to speak.

His voice is soft, not strained and not shouting like so many other teachers you have heard, but it fills the grove completely, every word reaching the ears of the audience. His eyes, caught in the light of the oil lamps, twinkle, radiating his message of love and compassion. With an expression of infinite serenity he gazes at the assembled crowd, until his eyes fall on you.

With the softest of smiles and inclining his body slightly in your direction he speaks, and you, knowing that his words are meant just for your ears, compose yourself and allow them to reach the very heart of your being.

"Everything begins in our mind. It is the action of our mind that determines what we do and how we live. Mind is the most important part of our being. If we speak or act with a mind that is filled with greed or hatred or moods and emotions that cause other people unhappiness, then we too can never be truly happy. The unpleasant results of these actions will follow us as the wheel follows the ox that draws the cart.

But when we can free our mind from the sway of greed and hatred we will feel our life to be more precious. We will be happier and also able to share this happiness with all the other beings we come into contact with. This happiness, based in love and compassion is like your shadow in the brightest part of the day. Unshakable.

If we carry with us thoughts of ill will and animosity towards others we are always far from the truth. To let go of these kinds of thoughts and feelings will not only bring us closer to the truth but also take us to a real and lasting happiness.

It has been said from ages past, that hatred is never overcome by more hatred and that only love can overcome hatred. This is an eternal law.

Everywhere, people who are not wise fight and quarrel believing that in some way they and everything they support and stand for will last for ever.

My friends, we must all come to death one day and so give up all we have fought to retain. How can it be other than this? Those who realise this simple truth will no longer fight with others.

As rain will penetrate the roof of a house that has been poorly finished, so too will the passions that lead to unhappiness penetrate the mind that is not protected by the development of concentration, insight and love.

But also in the same way as rain cannot penetrate a roof that is well finished, the development of concentration, insight and love will repel the conditions that are not conducive to happiness.

To train in moral restraint and to cultivate the mind through the practice of meditation is the way to end the suffering, discontent and unhappiness we all experience, simply because we are alive.

The purpose of the holy life is to benefit oneself and others through our speech and actions but more importantly, to purify the mind from the taints of greed, hatred and delusion, the three fires that burn within us all.

This path of purification can be followed by anyone who has a heart that wants to be free, and to them the results are assured. This beautiful way has been realised by me and I offer this path to any who will give themselves to it.

May you all be well and happy, and may you come to realise

for yourselves this Path of Purification."

As the words fade, the deep silence returns to the grove. You sit at peace in the stillness of the night. The words have burned deep into your heart, and you feel almost weak from the effect of them. In front of you the Buddha and his attendants stand easily with grace and elegance, and glide gently and silently back into the darkness.

You have received the words of an enlightened being of that you are sure.
You now know that your life can never be the same. In your mind is only the space left by the wisdom of the words. No decisions or plans can be made until this wisdom has been fully appreciated.
The people around you begin to move and whispers and coughing intrude upon the quietness that had been so deeply felt. Slowly, you get to your feet and join the others already moving off. Families head in the direction of the town, one or two of the younger men walk into the darkness, following the steps of the Buddha.

You watch them, but you don't join them.
Not this time.
Perhaps one day, even soon, but not this day.

For you, it is enough to have heard the words of an enlightened being. Now it is time for reflection and contemplation. As you walk with the crowd towards the lights of the town, you are approached by people, some already met by you, wanting to know what you thought of the talk and how you feel.

They are asking if your journey was necessary.

You only want to be silent and alone, but you have to answer.
For you now, it is still time to be a part of the world.

> It is good to respect
> wise people in the world,
> whether they are masters or disciples,
> if they have overcome
> all obstacles to their own illumination.
> To offer respect to such beings
> brings benefits
> that cannot be measured.

Dhammapada: verses 195 &196

PART THREE

Questions and Answers

Not This

Questions and Answers

'The point of practice is to know ourselves'

Question:
Why is it that I seem to have such a problem with anger?

Answer:
It's interesting to notice the words we use to describe certain things, because it is our language that defines our relationship to a particular situation. As soon as we used the word 'problem', we have created a situation of conflict. We have in our mind an ideal scenario of how things should be for us all the time, and in this instance there is no room for anger.
Anger is a natural state of mind, based in ignorance. As long as we have ignorance, we always have the potential for anger, and so we have to have the awareness that it can arise in any moment. Throughout this life, and possibly many lifetimes before, our tendencies towards anger have gone unchecked. A situation occurs, we become angry and then react. This is a natural manifestation of the ignorant mind. Sometimes, of course, we don't allow the anger to show because we repress it. We force it down into what is called the 'subconscious or unconscious mind', where it simmers away for some time until eventually as must happen, it comes bursting forth with all the force of a nuclear weapon. Often the object for that anger is something trivial, but even so, it is a condition for us to vent our unconscious feelings.
So, anger is a habit, and now you expect it to stop just because you have a meditation practice. But consider, if you're a smoker and you stop smoking do you still crave for a cigarette? Even if you are very strong and don't give in to

these cravings, they still arise. Our habits, conditioned in the past, will appear now. Even if we don't prompt them.

Wanting a cigarette even though you have actually stopped smoking is a common situation and noticing the presence of anger is no different. Habits from the past arising now.

Of course, our training is to be aware of the mental state of anger, without actually giving in to it and becoming angry. This takes skill, and no one should be blamed for weakening to it sometimes, but here as with everything, we need to use wisdom.

Actually, there is nothing wrong with anger at all. In the moment when anger arises, look at it. No need to justify, rationalise or explain it, to see it is enough. A habit arising from the past. Notice the effect in the body. How do you really experience this particular mental state? Forget fighting and blaming someone else, take your attention to the body state and just be with it. Relax and let it pass. It will be very interesting for you, I think.

But how do we do this?

The first thing we have to do is remove ourselves from the situation. Not dramatically by slamming doors or making an unkind remark, but quietly and peacefully seeing this as a moment for training. Then find a quiet spot and simply be with it. Sometimes, if the energy is too strong, a long walk will help, but don't waste your time searching for someone to blame. Your anger comes from you, not someone else. Only you can remedy it.

So, you see that anger is not a problem, it is an opportunity to train and see something in a new way. But you have to be brave and determined and not allow ego to interfere. Once ego is involved, it is fighting for itself. It is the ego that needs someone to blame for everything that doesn't go according to its plans, and ego that feels the need to explain and justify its every action.

Actually, there is no need to say anything. If you're angry just notice that, it's enough. To say I'm angry 'because of you', is already too much.

Anger, as with all mental states, presents itself without our calling. We are not responsible for it except by way of habit, and so should not see it as a problem, only a wonderful opportunity to train.

Take the long view. We have to deal with this habit sometime, it might as well be now, so use this moment.

As we notice our habits and tendencies from the past arising into the present moment we have the opportunity to let them go. To let them all go. Anger, hatred, desires and all the rest. Until they show themselves to us, we can't do anything.

Vipassana is not a system of repression. It is a way to face all the unpleasant qualities that manifest in your life, due to ignorance and propel you always in a certain direction.

Learn to see them not as problems, but only as wonderful opportunities to free yourself from their grasp. Without our anger, how could we be free from our anger?

Question:
But doesn't that mean we just have to give in to what someone else wants or demands?

Answer:
When we give in to anger, we become ugly and irrational. We no longer have a clear view of the situation. We are just lost in the heat of the moment. In this condition, we can say and do things that are hurtful both to ourselves and to others. Anger, no matter how justified it may seem at the time, actually has no beneficial qualities. The Buddha has said that

in the face of an enemy, we are already defeated when we display anger. To understand the situation properly, we need a cool head. This comes from balance and not being drawn into extremes. Under these circumstances, people are less likely to take advantage of you because you are always in control of your responses.

This raises another interesting point.
Many people feel that because they are involved in a meditation practice such as Vipassana and loving kindness and try to follow a lifestyle of harmony and love for our fellow beings, these principles are always being taken advantage of. Because they don't want to fight, they find themselves submitting to the whims of others. There is absolutely no need for this to occur. If you don't want to do something, just don't do it. If you feel someone is trying to take advantage of you, don't let them. State your case quietly and simply and then let it go. There is no need to go into great detail, or resort to anger. Just say what you feel. Stay centred, and stay in control, but don't allow yourself to be a victim. This doesn't help anyone.

We have to remember that as long as others are spiritually ignorant, their words and actions will always betray them, and the result of this can only be further unhappiness.
We however, are training ourselves on the path of wisdom and love by breaking our old habits and conditioning and allowing a clear and more beautiful way of living to develop. Sometimes we have to be very strong in difficult circumstances, but that strength must come from wisdom, and the conviction that we do what we do for the benefit of all, otherwise it is just more selfish action. Yours or someone else's. And the result can only be more and more ego in the

world.

Have confidence in yourself and your practice and remember, you may not always know what you want, but you always know what you don't want. Listen to these feelings and honour them. Take the opportunity to cultivate wisdom by seeing the mind for what it really is and realise for yourself where it can take you without awareness, but don't condemn those who can't.

Question:
You say that we are 'not the body and not the mind', are you going to tell us what we are?

Answer:
(laughing) Good question.
When I said this one time somebody answered 'the self', but what does that mean?
When we use terms like 'soul' or 'self', they are just more ideas, more fantasy.
What exactly is this 'soul' or 'self' and where can we find it? As long as we have not experienced the source of the mind we are always caught up in concepts and belief.
The Tao te Ching tells us that 'the Tao that can be named is not the eternal Tao'.
Once something can be identified and labelled it becomes limited. If it is limited, it is not eternal. That which is 'not body' and 'not mind', cannot be named or described but it can be experienced. It can be known. Knowing is the point of practice. With knowing comes the falling away of the small mind that needs to grasp and cling to labels.
Language is always limiting. We can never really say what we mean, sometimes we can't even get close. How much truer is this with the depth of spiritual pursuit?

So, let go of trying to find out what you are and see what you are not.
You're not the body and you're not the mind.
Be open. Don't label, don't identify, simply be.

Question:
What exactly is insight?

Answer:
Insight is knowing. It is a direct experience of the truth. Just that.
The experience of insight can arise at any time. It is not confined to formal meditation practice. It can happen when you brush your teeth, are walking to the shops or eating your soup. Anytime.
But this also raises a good point.
In all the years I have been travelling to different groups and sharing Dhamma, no one has ever reacted to the things I have said by exclaiming, 'Is that really true?'
The truths I outline are obvious ones and once pointed out, seem clear and simple. In fact, we can say that truth itself is not remarkable, it is only the obvious.
Just before the Buddha died, Ananda, his cousin and his loving attendant, went to him and said, "Master, the monks have gathered to be with you before you die, will you not give them one last teaching?"
The Buddha replied, "Ananda what more can I say? I have not had the closed fist of some teachers."
This means that the Buddha did not hold any part of the truth or his teachings in reserve. It was and is, available to all, monks and nuns, laymen and laywomen. Each has equal opportunity to study and each has equal opportunity for liberation. This truth is not something special or academically reserved for

those who are more intelligent than others. On the contrary, it is for everyone and can be seen all around us.

In Vipassana there is no secret teaching.

So, I say to you, 'You are not the body and you are not the mind'. At first, this may sound a little extreme, because we have always lived as though we are the body and we are the mind, but when we eventually examine this statement with detachment and wisdom, we begin to understand the truth of it. Actually, it seems so obvious that we wonder how it is possible that we have not seen it before.

This body is not yours. This mind is not yours. Neither will do only what we want them to, and both only do what they do.

If the mind was 'ours' we would always be happy, if the body was 'ours' we would never be sick, or get old or die. This direct realisation of the truth we call insight.

It is not an intellectual appreciation. It is direct knowing. And the result of this direct knowing can never be lost or forgotten, because insight is not the getting of something; it is a losing! A losing of a piece of ignorance or non-understanding of the truth that determines our life. This means that everything we think, do or say from that moment onwards will be affected by this loss. Our thoughts, actions and speech will be purer as our insights develop and deepen.

But we also have to remember that our habits and levels of ignorance go very deep indeed, and one small experience of insight will not eradicate them completely. This process can take time. A lot of time. But we have to continue, allowing the resulting purity of mind to grow and slowly, slowly eradicate the reservoir of ignorance.

For this to happen, we must continue our practice. One small insight is not complete enlightenment, but by continuing on the path, it will happen. Once the process has begun it's hard

to stop.
So keep reflecting 'I'm not the body and I'm not the mind'[2]. This statement will lead to more and more insights and these insights will lead to the deepest levels of understanding.

Question:
You say that by doing this practice, not only will I benefit, but ultimately all beings. I find it hard to accept that my meditation practice can be of use to people living in war-torn countries or facing starvation through political upheaval.

Answer:
Think about it. What is the root cause of all the problems in the world? It's ignorance, isn't it? Men and women acting from selfish desires to create their own particular kind of life, often at the expense of the feelings of others. This is politics and religion, and even with the best of intentions, without wisdom, it's just another manifestation of ego.
We always think that we know what is right for ourselves and for others, and will sometimes go to great lengths to enforce that view. Often, as we can already see in the world, this means inflicting great pain and suffering upon one group of people or beings, in order to promote the welfare of another. If we want to see the direct manifestation of spiritual ignorance, just look in the world.

Do you think that someone like Hitler thought he was wrong? Of course not. He believed his view of the future world was exactly right and so put the plan into operation to realise it.

---

2   The Vipassana koan, a modern interpretation of the Anattalakhana Sutta , the marks of No-Self.

This plan brought about the deaths and suffering of millions of beings, but that was the cost and presumably to Hitler, worth every life.

This is how the unenlightened person behaves in the world, through acts of selfishness that ultimately knows no bounds. Even democracy is flawed. It works on the principle of fear and greed. Vote for me and I'll give you what you want, vote for the other and you will lose something you would like to keep.

So even our attitude towards voting in elections is based only on our selfish desires to get what we want for ourselves. Sometimes, it has to be said, our motivation is much higher than financial or personal reward, and we may want to see the establishment of a true welfare state, where everything can be shared. Our own view of Utopia.

But here, as always, we have to be aware. Our view of what is right will rarely be the same as everybody else's. Even inside religious groups and political parties, there are many wings and factions all fighting to promote their own particular view of how things should be.

We have to understand that utopia is a dream that will never be realised. Man's basic ignorance will see to that. There will always be someone with a different opinion to you and ready to fight for it. And what is it that we really fight about? Ideas, only ideas.

We fight about whose craziness is best!

So how does your meditation practice help the situation? How can others benefit?

We can say that by living a natural and spiritual lifestyle you are already contributing to the welfare of others, simply by not harming them, or stealing from them or becoming involved in sexual misconduct and by not using your speech in cruel and harmful ways.

From these simple actions of restraint you are bringing enormous benefit to the world. Even if you are not actively doing good, at the lowest level you are not doing harm.

You're not making world matters worse. Added to this list of moral behaviour, we can include the absence of intoxicating liquor or drugs that tend to cloud the mind. With a clear head, at least on the conventional level, we can be more receptive about what needs to be done in different situations.

But this still isn't wisdom. This is simply moral behaviour. How to live in the world without causing harm to oneself and others. Wisdom comes from meditation practice. By recognising the real nature of mind and body. When we know at the intuitive or heart level, that thoughts, moods, feelings and emotions arise and pass away without end, we have a different perspective on how to live in the world. We don't need to intimately know every person that lives, we only need to know ourselves. The moment we know ourselves, we spontaneously know others.

Your pain, your thoughts, your moods, your feelings and your emotions are exactly the same as my pain, my thoughts, my moods, my feelings and my emotions. There are not billions of separate beings living in the world. There is only one. One living being with one heart and one mind.

Pain for you is exactly the same as pain for me. Pleasant feelings for you are exactly the same as pleasant feelings for me. No difference. Only the objects are different. What frightens you may not frighten me, but when fear arises in either of us, it is the same experience.

One teacher said it like this,

> 'The greatest delusion that faces mankind
> is that you're out there and I'm in here'.

Very beautiful. When we are able to let go of the destructive sense of separateness, we understand the oneness and interconnectedness of all things. So, by knowing ourselves, we know everything. All living things. Human beings, animals, birds, fish, insects, nature itself.

This knowledge brings with it positive changes in our way of living as the understanding of the dangerous potential of ignorance deepens. It affects everything we do. We begin to naturally respond to situations, not through selfish desires of wanting everything done our way but rather through wisdom and harmony. Of doing whatever is appropriate, and flowing with the situation.

Sometimes this may mean going out into the world and being of service to others, or it may mean living quietly, perhaps raising a family and instilling into them values that will help the world in the future. This of course must be done by example and not through indoctrination.

All the problems of the world begin with ignorance, or as another great teacher once put it,

> 'There are no problems in the world -
> you are the problem!'

Anyone who is truly engaged in the cultivation of wisdom through the eradication of ignorance is already helping every living being that we share this planet with.

Question:
Do we have to destroy our ego?

Answer:
What is ego? What is it that we have to destroy? When we

look for ego, where do we look? Where can we find it?
Ego is not something tangible like an arm or a leg, something that we can see or feel. Ego is really just a series of misunderstandings about ourselves. It is the manifestation of ignorance in our lives. Ego is only the momentary identification with this mind and body as being who and what we really are. Ego is the place where our suffering begins, and is also the place where we experience that suffering. In this respect, we have to destroy it, eradicate it completely, but not through violence or intolerance, but only through love. We have to love this ego to death!

We have to be gentle with ourselves, take our time and allow the power of the ego to simply fall away. This is done by recognising it whenever it appears and no longer feeding it. We don't have to fight it and there is no need to make it the enemy. When we see ego as the enemy we simply divide the mind into the part we want, and the part we definitely don't want. Really, there is just mind, manifesting moment after moment. No need for conflict.

When the Buddha was asked about this, he said that the best way to put out a fire is to simply not add any more fuel to it. To let it burn out by itself. This is how we must be. When ego appears in whatever form, just recognise it and let it go. That way, the power of ego is taken away and peace is attained.

When we use terms like 'destroy', 'kill' and 'annihilate', with regard to the ego, it does not display much loving kindness, and as long as we think like this we will live in a state of conflict, making an enemy of our own mind.

So live in peace with the ego and allow it to be. Don't indulge it but allow it to be, don't repress it but allow it to be. Don't feed it, but don't deny it. When it arises just know it. Be kind, loving, and let it go. See the whole mind as it is, an endless stream of thoughts, moods, feelings and emotions and none

of them are you. The pleasant ones are not you, neither are the unpleasant ones. So let them go, let them all go.
Letting go is the way to peace. It is the way to live happily with yourself, and consequently the whole world. With this practice of loving awareness, we can change everything. We don't need to destroy anything. Everything will take care of itself.

Question:
You say that 'practice is everything', but isn't that just selfishness?

Answer:
When the Buddha was dying, one monk decided that it would be better for him to continue his practice of meditation in the hills rather than to join the other monks at the Buddhas camp, waiting for the death to occur. When the Buddha heard about this he praised that monks attitude, pointing out that he knew what was valuable, and what was not.
Practice is everything.
With practice, we empty ourselves of the impurities of greed, hatred and the confusion that blinds us to the reality of life. In the Theravada tradition of Buddhism, this is called the Vishudhimagga, the path of purification.
When we see clearly the natural tendencies of mind, we will notice that they are established firmly in our own selfish desire for happiness. We pursue this happiness blindly, often hurting others in the process, simply by not knowing the depth of what we do. Once we are living with love and awareness as our foundation for life, we can see what is beneficial to ourselves and others and what is not. As long as we don't know how things are, we will always be acting from a position based in ignorance. Simply contributing

more confusion to an already confused world.

Question:
What about God?

Answer:
Actually, the question of God isn't something we need to concern ourselves with.
If we think back to the moment we awoke this morning and trace the events of the day until this moment now we can see that some good things happened, and some not so good things happened, and in any event, things turned out as they did.
Now, if we tell ourselves that God exists, these things happened. If we tell ourselves that God does not exist, these things happened anyway.
Whether God exists or not, does not alter our life in any way, and forming an opinion or taking a position for or against his reality, does not help us on our spiritual quest. The road to liberation must be free from blind faith and belief.
We can only ever know what we know, and keep an open mind about the rest.

Question:
You have talked about belief, but isn't it important to have something to believe in?

Answer:
We have to be careful here not to be confused by the use of language and the different natures of belief.
In religious terms belief means blind faith. It means accepting something as being true, when in reality, we don't know whether it is or not. So, some people believe that God is one

thing whilst others believe that he or even she, is something else, but they don't know for themselves. Their belief is based upon what they have read, or what they have heard, or what they have been told and they, due to subtle mental feelings, accept these things as being true. Even after much thought and discussion, so overwhelming are the subtle mental feelings that even the most illogical beliefs can be adhered to. Outside religion there are also many beliefs. Flying saucers, alien abductions, the Loch Ness monster and many, many more. The list goes on, but the point is that as human beings we have a mind that can believe in anything.

But we only believe in things that we don't know from our own direct experience, and belief is not the truth. Belief is what we cultivate when we don't know the truth.

Now, as a guiding principle of life, we can say that we believe in love and awareness through the practice of meditation, but here we use the word in a different way. If we apply these trainings to our life and consequently experience the results, it cannot be called belief. It is knowing based upon direct experience.

The intention behind spiritual practice is to go beyond the realm of belief and realise the truth for ourselves. In the meantime, there are so many things yet to be understood, we should keep an open mind and not take positions either for or against them.

Question:
If I wanted to achieve quick results, what would I have to do?

Answer:
Basically you would have to give up that very ambition. The desire to get something blinds you to where you already are. If the minds natural state is already pure, where are you

trying to go? What are you trying to get?

The practice here is to see where we are, accept that as a starting point and begin to build. We don't have to destroy everything and replace it with something else. We must work with what we have.

In the meditation we watch the breath, everything else follows from that. The first thing to learn is how to observe the body as it breathes, not how to experience the more subtle elements of matter that make up our physical form. When we are able to watch the breath with the right attitude we will naturally be able to obtain deeper levels of awareness.

One thing leads to the next.

From this we will be able to understand mind and body, our own human nature, as it is. The Japanese say that 'water boils quickly, but it must be on the heat for a long time'. This means that although insight always arises in an instant, the preparation for it may have been taking place for a very long time. It is not possible to know when insights will arise, but by practicing with the right attitude, it will happen.

Question:
So what is the right attitude?

Answer:
Simply doing the practice for its own sake, and not for something you think you can get from it. In other words, sitting just to sit.

We all know now that in meditation we cannot control the mental states. They come and go as they choose and not as we decide. However, once we surrender into this reality and no longer resist, we can experience the peacefulness of a mind in harmony with itself. We can be at ease with, and learn from, whatever mental state presents itself to us, not only in the meditation, but in every moment of life. This is practicing with the right attitude.

Question:
I find I am very selfish and have many desires. What shall I do?

Answer:
The first thing to do is not to be too hard on yourself. This is how it is to everyone.
We all want to be happy and we attempt to realise that happiness through our desires. These desires manifest as wanting things we think will make us happy, and annihilating or getting rid of things we feel are making us unhappy. This is the usual way of living for most people.
However, here we have begun to train ourselves. We have begun to see what lies behind the desire and what we can do about it. Having the desire is not the important part, desires come and go, what we can do about them is.
For you, your training has started because you already notice this movement of mind. You are putting some space between your mental impulse of getting something and the act of doing it. You have begun to break the habit of blind reaction and develop the wisdom of response. Doing, whatever is appropriate in a given situation.
What you can do about it is keep on practicing. Let go of ambition and simply keep on doing exactly what you're doing.
If you see the biggest piece of cake on the plate and you want it, just notice that mental impulse and respond. Either take it or leave it as you like.
The most important thing here is awareness and not making

a problem out of our natural tendencies of mind. Just relax, observe them and do the right thing.

May all beings be happy

Acknowledgements

No book ever writes itself, and although the idea always seems simple, the actual work of sharing ones thoughts in a coherent way demands the help of others.
In this respect I feel blessed to have been aided by the people listed below, for their help, support and expertise.
Peter Mayrhofer and Olga Trucios for their support, advice and final proof reading of this version.
Isabelle Kewley, my wife, supporter and friend, who typeset the words and made them into the book you are reading.
To all my students and disciples for their encouragement to continually make the Pure Dhamma available so that all beings may benefit.
To these people and others I have not mentioned, I am as always, extremely grateful.
May they all be well and happy

About the author

Michael Kewley is the former Buddhist monk Paññadipa, who is now an internationally acclaimed Master of Dhamma, presenting courses and meditation retreats throughout the world. For many years he was the guiding teacher at the International Meditation Centre, Budh Gaya, India and is the founder of the Pure Dhamma tradition of spiritual awakening and the Being Awake meditation group network.

A disciple of the late Sayadaw Rewata Dhamma, he teaches solely on the instruction of his own Master; to share the Dhamma, in the spirit of the Buddha, so that all beings might benefit. On 26th May 2002, during a special ceremony at the Dhamma Talaka Temple in England, he was awarded the title of Dhammachariya.

A full biography of Michael Kewley, including videos and Dhamma talk extracts, can be found at:

www.puredhamma.org

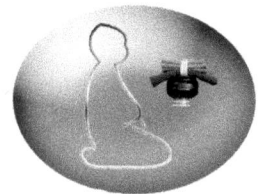

Also by Michael Kewley

Published by
Panna Dipa Books

Higher than Happiness
Vipassana – the way to an awakened life
Life Changing Magic
Walking the Path
The Other Shore
Life is not Personal
Nimm das Leben nicht persönlich
The Reality of Kamma
Buttons in the Dana Box
Knöpfe in der Dana Box
The Dhammapada

Not This

www.ingramcontent.com/pod-product-compliance
Lightning Source LLC
Chambersburg PA
CBHW051105160426
43193CB00010B/1329